REFRAMING
GENERATIONAL
STEREOTYPES

**Embrace Age Diversity,
Build Mutual Understanding
and Foster Collaboration to
Drive Positive Change**

REFRAMING
GENERATIONAL
STEREOTYPES

Embrace Age Diversity,
Build Mutual Understanding
and Foster Collaboration to
Drive Positive Change

RACHELE FOCARDI

Mc
Graw
Hill

REFRAMING GENERATIONAL STEREOTYPES
Embrace Age Diversity, Build Mutual Understanding and Foster Collaboration to Drive Positive Change

The Internet addresses listed in the text were accurate at the time of publication. The inclusion of a website does not indicate an endorsement by the authors or McGraw-Hill Education, and McGraw-Hill Education does not guarantee the accuracy of the information presented at these sites.

Cover design by Dragan Bilic

1 2 3 4 5 6 7 8 9 10 SLP 23 22 21 20

When ordering this title, use **ISBN 978-981-4923-09-5 or MHID 981-4923-09-5**

Printed in Singapore

Note from the Author

While writing this book, I have seen a rising number of articles and videos claiming *"generations may not exist"*, *"there is no such thing as generational divide"* or *"generational differences are not real"*. Instead, they reinforce that *"people are people"* and it is wrong to group us under a generational umbrella. Although the underlying message is an honorable one, this notion is reductive, and those propagating it — while surely meaning well — may be doing more harm than good. Let me explain why. While it is true that we are all unique individuals and should not be victims of bias, it is also undoubtably true that the context we are born and raised in (socio-economic, historical, political, cultural, even technological) shapes us. In a similar way, context defines generations.

The reality a Traditionalist, a Baby Boomer or a Gen X experienced upon entering the workforce — including behavioral norms, management styles, what defined leadership, how people were developed, and how they interacted — is different than what it is today. So are parenting styles, communication styles, and social customs. Hence, there are inevitably attitudes, ways of thinking, expectations and modi operandi shared among those who were born, raised, entered adulthood and joined the workforce during the same time period.

Failing to acknowledge this is a big contributor to intergenerational conflicts. **Generational Diversity is Diversity**. It is difficult to understand and appreciate differences, or show sensibility in how we interact with other age groups, if we flat out refuse to acknowledge the many forces that have shaped them. Encouraging deep cross-generational awareness (instead of dismissing the need for it), openly addressing, challenging, reframing — and perhaps, in some ways, even embracing — the stereotype, is the only way to bridge the generational divide and foster a culture of Intergenerational Collaboration.

I also want to address the cultural aspect. I am often asked whether generational trends are consistent around the world, or whether they are just broad generalizations. Generations are defined by largescale events. Prior to Millennials, generations emerged across different parts of the world at different times, and many defining generational traits varied from region to region — even country to country. This was not solely due to dissimilar socio-economic realities. Until the late 1990s, the world was still relatively "siloed" and young people in one country did not know much — or anything at all — about what their peers across the globe were living and experiencing. In short, there was little information transfer. This is why the Millennial Generation "came into existence" in North America ("Ground Zero") in 1981 but, according to a number of generational studies, did not reach Europe and Asia until approximately 1986.

Globalization and Technology, however, have bridged generation gaps between countries and cultures, both in terms of time and defining characteristics. Millennials and Gen Z grew up in a prolonged period of peace and relative uniformity, with free flow of information and people. The emergence of a connected world with correlated economic trends, content, and Internet pop-culture led to generations developing relatively similar mind-sets and values that, in turn, led to strong global cohesiveness.

Hence, today, even as we stand in a period of regionalization as a form of deglobalization, we can confidently assume that many of the traits that define Millennials and Gen Z are relatively consistent across most developed and emerging markets. While these are the traits I will be focusing on, I still ask that you leave some wiggle room to account for dominant cultural idiosyncrasies.

Introduction

As we enter the 2020s, we have a growingly age-diverse workforce due to half a century of fluctuating birth rates alongside increased life expectancy. With older generations working past the age of retirement and the arrival of Gen Z, we are seeing for the first time in history four — sometimes five — generations working alongside each other. As a result, many organizations are experiencing the **X-Y-Z Divide Syndrome**, where Generational Diversity is seen as a negative element, making it more difficult to build and maintain a happy productive workplace. At the same time, our world is facing unprecedented crises — from Environmental and Social to the Covid-19 Pandemic — that will require the ability to harness the power of our collective strengths. It has never been more important than it **is right now** for the older generations to take the young under their wings, listen to them, enable them, and empower them to change the world by innovating and driving impact.

While organizations strive to convey a harmonious and supportive working culture, underlying intergenerational conflicts prevent employees belonging to different age groups from collaborating positively and effectively. Baby Boomers and Gen X often disapprove of *what they view as* entitlement and lack of commitment on the part of the younger generations, so they fail to provide the mentorship and empowerment that young employees crave. As a result, Millennials and Gen Z feel unheard and unable to contribute, and blame the top-down management style and "old-school" mindset of the older generations.

At the same time, Baby Boomers and Gen X, who have years of experience under their belt, are dismayed to find — as digital natives whizz right past them — that their years of hard work and invaluable industry knowledge no longer guarantee advancement. Yet, Millennials and Gen Z do not *seem* to appreciate the freedom and the many opportunities they are given, nor — to add insult to injury — do they *seem* to value their older colleagues' experience, or respect their position. All this intensifies discord among workers and leads to low employee engagement, higher attrition, stagnated innovation and a weakened Employer Brand.

What it boils down to is a lack of mutual understanding and awareness of the forces that shaped each generation. Baby Boomers, Gen X, Millennials and Gen Z have different mindsets, expectations and respond differently to varying communication styles, yet they have one thing in common: **They ALL feel misunderstood.** Appreciating each other's needs, viewpoints, strengths, weaknesses, challenges — even fears — is key to unlocking the power of Intergenerational Collaboration.

Acknowledgments

First and foremost, to **Victor**, the love of my life and my North Star. Throughout life's storms you have remained relentlessly by my side, showing me the way, encouraging me, and supporting me. Everything that matters in my world today would not have been possible without you.

I also want to acknowledge three extraordinary people who have — knowingly or unknowingly — put me on the path towards writing this book. **Kerrianne Lim Joon**, for your trust and friendship throughout the years, **Bob Aubrey**, for your mentorship and guidance, and **Jennifer Ting**, for being an early adopter and advocate of positive Intergenerational Collaboration.

My profound gratitude goes out to my mother, **Francesca**, and to my best friend, **Marisa**. If I chose this time and space, it is most definitely because I knew I would find you here. Thank you for your love, once again.

To my children **Luna**, **Trayan** and **Mira**. You are all that is beautiful in this world. I have so much faith and confidence in what you will be able to accomplish. Just like Bastian in *The Neverending Story*, you hold in the palm of your hands the magic, love and wisdom needed to build a whole new world, one that will surely be better — if not only, from you being in it.

To Maria Consuelo Arafol Sumobay — **"Cici"** — for everything.

Finally, to all the people who have contributed to this book by sharing their experiences, **thank you for telling me your story**.

Rachele

Foreword

Every generation worries about the next and yet, so far, each new generation has always changed things for the better. As we enter the Fourth Industrial Revolution, once again major transformative changes are inevitable.

Knowledge used to be power. Now knowledge is a commodity easily available on the Internet, often for free. As computing powers advance rapidly, automation, robotization and algorithms are now replacing labor at a rapid pace. Every sector of society is due for disruption. If employers can use robots, will they prefer not to employ humans? If machine learning can make things cheaper, faster, better and easier, who needs us? What must we do to prepare our young for what is to come? Rachele's book offers us deep insights into the future and how we can prepare and even create it through **the power of Intergenerational Collaboration**.

The reality is, it is not the technologies we should be worried about. They are transient; they, too, will become obsolete and be replaced by newer ones. And new technologies appear because someone has imagination and vision. What is constant is our ability to create and mobilize them as they emerge. This means that beyond hard skills, what we desperately need are "human skills" such as:

- Curiosity to question;
- Courage to imagine and implement;
- Commitment to complete challenging and tedious tasks;

- Compassion to empathize with all people: customers, colleagues, bosses, and the world at large. The power of love is infectious to boosting teamwork;

- Collaboration. The ability to mobilize others into win-win alignments;

- Community circumspection, so as to be able to use an "ecosystem approach" to solutions, instead of thinking only in fragmented silo views; and

- Communication skills to inform, equip and motivate actions by others.

Gen Z offer us a promising future. They care for the environment, they demand social justice, better distribution of wealth, peace and prosperity for all. To bring forth the world they envisage, we need to move from competition to collaboration; from silo solutions to ecosystem thinking; having both specialized and diverse skills. As such, we need to create an educational revolution away from grades and rote learning.

Covid-19 has driven us to cut unnecessary consumption, travel, pollution, and has taught us family bonding. As we recover from the Covid-19 Pandemic in the coming years, I hope we will return to a new future where we redefine a Billionaire as one who improves the lives of a billion people, and not one who hoards money.

I have full confidence that our future will be bright because — as a Baby Boomer who works daily with Millennials and Gen Z — I am deeply impressed by their sense of care for our planet, people and animals. Indeed, we need to return to nature to use biomimicry as a model for our society. In a simple leaf, we can learn irrigation, energy distribution, management structures, engineering, arts, biology, communication, and a never-ending list as long as our curiosity.

We need to return to a Purpose, one which we each must individually define.

I am very impressed by Rachele's understanding of the minds of our young people, and the way she incites all of us to help them shape our future into a much better one. As Rachele advocates, it is indeed our responsibility to guide them, not just at home, but at school and in the workplace. And we need to start NOW.

This book will illustrate how each of us can leverage our own unique strengths, and by reframing generational stereotypes, work collaboratively to become catalysts for positive change. I know you will enjoy reading it as much as I did.

Jack Sim
Baby Boomer, Philanthropist, Entrepreneur
Founder of the World Toilet Organization

About the Author

Rachele Focardi is a global thought-leader and world-renowned public speaker on Multigenerational Workforce Dynamics, *The Future of Work*, Employer Branding and Talent Strategy. Born and raised in Italy, she spent her professional life between Europe, U.S.A. and Asia.

Since 2003, Rachele has spearheaded the Employer Branding movement globally, advocating that organizations and governments incorporate an Employer Branding Strategy into their workforce planning. Over the years she has advised hundreds of Fortune 500 companies, Asian organizations, NGOs and Government Agencies on how to launch their Employer Branding practices at home and abroad.

Today, Rachele's passion is to help organizations adapt to the needs of the new generations and make Generational Diversity a key item on their Diversity and Inclusion Agenda by developing strategies, initiatives and programs that provide the opportunity for employees across all age groups to learn *about* each other and *from* each other, collaborate effectively, and together drive change.

Rachele is also committed to helping Governments, Organizations and Education Systems undergoing transformation meet the needs of the future workforce.

After 12 years in the U.S.A. Rachele, who is a Gen X, moved to Singapore in 2011, where she lives with her husband Victor, a Millennial, and their three children, Luna, Trayan and Mira.

Rachele is the Chair of the Multigenerational Workforce Committee for the **ASEAN Human Development Organization**, Founder and CEO of **XYZ@Work**, and Mentor at **The Workplace Accelerator** and various other organizations. Previously Chief Strategy Officer APAC for Universum, Anchor and Network Correspondent for CFN-CNBC, Rachele is also a member of **MENSA**.

Contact Rachele

www.xyzatwork.com

Contents

Part 1 — How Effectively Leading a Multigenerational Workforce Became a Business Priority

Part 2   The Multigenerational Workforce — From Baby Boomers to Gen Z

Part 3   Winning Strategies and Initiatives to Harness the Power of Intergenerational Collaboration

PART 1

How Effectively Leading a Multigenerational Workforce Became a Business Priority

"Every new generation is a fresh invasion of savages."
Hervey Allen

Chapter 1

Why This Book is REALLY Important — A Gen X Story

The topic of this book is very close to my heart. It is the product of 20 years of experiences across different life stages and continents, working with hundreds of employers and educational institutions, and talking to thousands of students and professionals from around the world. I like to believe the tiny seed that blossomed into my deep love for helping bridge the generational divide was planted in 2001 when I moved back to Italy after graduating from a top Journalism program in the U.S.A.

I had chosen to major in communications because I loved using words to help people "see" things; I even believed I would one day become a war correspondent and win a Pulitzer Prize. Like most high school graduates back then, I hadn't given much thought to my choice of degree. It was something we were told we needed, but were provided little context about what career we could have by choosing one course of study over another. Mostly because, frankly, it wouldn't make much difference. In a country with an average youth unemployment rate of 30 percent and no appreciation for young talent, getting a job — any job — was considered a blessing. It did not matter whether it matched our interests, whether it had anything to do with what we studied, or whether it was even paid. Most young graduates feared remaining unemployed and would do anything — even work for free or under ambiguous contract terms — in order to gain experience and put their minds to good use. Sadly, this seldom happened. They were, instead, mostly deployed on menial and boring tasks, with little opportunity to learn or grow.

My decision to move back to Italy drove a lifelong wedge between my father and me. I remember him telling me that it would be the biggest mistake of my life. I would be giving up a bright future and never be allowed to shine because, in Italy, drive and ambition were seldom rewarded. He may have had a point, but like many young adults, I took my chances and followed my heart. Finding a job proved even harder than I had imagined, and without my father's financial and emotional support, I was left to figure out how to make something of myself in a context I knew little about.

After a few rejections (I was too young, too inexperienced, too confident, too ambitious), I went to a temp agency and got a term contract with a large international advertising agency. Here, I experienced first-hand the dreadful working environment and the (not-so) subtle psychological abuse that young people had to endure from older colleagues in order to "build their bones". I will add more color to this in later chapters, the point is, it is this experience that set the wheels in motion for me. A year later, I started working for a local communication consulting company where one of my clients was Adcomms (today known as TMP Worldwide). My job was to give visibility to their "Employer Branding" campaigns. I had no idea initially what Employer Branding was, but once I learned there were organizations out there that not only paid their employees, but cared about them having a positive and rewarding work experience, I fell in love with it.

In 2005, after working as an anchorwoman for CNBC Class Financial Network in Milan, I moved back to the U.S.A. and started working at a leading Employer Branding company. It was here that I first got to know and understand Millennials. The company conducts an annual global study to understand what drives students' employment choices and what companies they want to work for. 2006 was an exceptional year. Because of the cutoff, most MBA students were Gen X and most undergraduate students were Millennials. When the survey results came out, I feared errors in the cleaning process; it seemed to be the only plausible way to justify such polar differences in the data sets: Gen X and Millennials wanted entirely different things! Once the results were confirmed, as a former public relations consultant and journalist, I realized the huge impact this mind frame shift from one generation to the next could have on the world if only it were amplified; and so, I contacted media, generational experts and academics, and started discovering an even stronger passion for helping employers adapt to the needs of this new generation. It is important to note, this was only a few years after a McKinsey study exposed "*The War for Talent*" as a strategic challenge and a critical driver of business success, and organizations were already struggling to differentiate themselves and attract the talent they needed. A supply–demand deficit coupled with an entire generation rising up and wanting things to change represented a unique opportunity. One I wanted to seize.

Since 2006, I have spearheaded the Employer Branding movement, advocating that organizations and governments incorporate an Employer Branding Strategy into their workforce planning. I have taken the desires and aspirations of the future workforce and have given them a voice. One by one, employers started understanding the importance of adapting to the needs of the new generation and began to reinvent themselves. For every organization that underwent this journey of transformation, thousands of employees and their families were positively affected. As industry and recruitment competitors started to follow suit, the number multiplied exponentially until most organizations around the world understood that a happy workforce is also a more productive one. Today (in certain countries, organizations and industries more than others) respect, well-being, flexibility, development, inclusion, friendliness can almost be taken for granted. In retrospect, by bringing the Millennial message to organizations around the world and supporting them in becoming better employers, I feel I have played a small part in changing the world.

This transformation, however, was not an easy one. Millennials dominated by numbers and it was clear to most that ignoring them was not an option. Almost overnight, the focus became on attracting, recruiting, engaging, developing and retaining them, causing a significant disruption within the existing workforce. Traditionalists, Baby Boomers and Gen X found themselves having to cater to this group of youngsters without understanding *why* they were getting "preferential treatment". After decades in the workforce, they were told to change their management styles, to show more patience and understanding, to rethink performance evaluation, and even to drop their academic performance requirements from their selection criteria because this new generation would be assessed differently. In no better words, Millennials were somewhat "shoved down their throats". And although seasoned employees had no choice but to adapt (for many, engaging Millennials and keeping them happy became a measurable KPI) they did not have to like it. And in fact, most did not.

This triggered a series of dynamics within the workforce that slowed down progress. Millennials arrived full of drive and ambition, and most organizations did not know how to handle it — or whether their fire should be fueled or contained. Existing employees started feeling demotivated as they watched Millennials walk in and enjoy treatment and recognition they could have only hoped to earn after years — if not decades — of hard work when they themselves first entered the workforce.

It was nobody's fault: in an effort to "win *The War for Talent*", organizations rushed to change without explaining to the existing workforce why these changes were necessary, why Millennials were different and why it was important that they be heard. Likewise, Millennials were not taught about existing workplace dynamics, about the forces that shaped their older managers and colleagues, and why their energy and ambition may meet resistance. The result was a conflicted workforce, where Millennials felt their drive was suppressed and where older generations found themselves having to cater to them without being fully onboard. It took years for the two to learn to work together, yet the rift is still there. This is because without a deep mutual understanding of the forces that shaped each age group, generations can learn how to coexist, but they will never fully embrace each other.

And now, Gen Z are the new Millennials, except the change they demand is not related to the working environment, but to an organization's genuine commitment to "do good". We are reading about their activism in the news every day. From Greta Thunberg's *"School Strike 4 Climate Action"* movement, the *#NeverAgain* Campaign to curb gun violence in the U.S.A., *#BlackLivesMatter* to protest against incidents of police brutality against African Americans, Malala Yousafzai and her quest to bring universal education to girls, more and more young people around the world are rising together behind a social cause. And here's the thing: our world desperately needs them. These teenagers full of tenacity and full of ideals must be encouraged and supported.

Like many of my peers, I came to terms with the fact that my generation will not be the one to change the world, but what Gen X can do is to guide Gen Z, and hand-in-hand with Millennials and Baby Boomers, enable them to drive impact and innovation. This cannot happen if upon entering the workforce a lack of mutual understanding prevents everyone from efficiently working together. It is now more important than ever for organizations to address the elephant in the room, shed light on the forces that shaped each generation, highlight strengths and similarities, and harmonize the Multigenerational Workforce behind common goals.

While reading this book, I encourage you to take a deep breath and go on an introspective journey through time to truly understand the context that each generation grew up in, and how it shaped their mindsets, their attitudes and their behaviors. I ask that you keep an open mind and an open heart. That you lower your guard and reflect on the stereotypes instead of rejecting them. That you try to imagine the power and innovation that can be unleashed when the vitality, creativity, and idealism of younger generations are combined with the knowledge, experience and resilience of older ones. And that you realize that we need to leverage our collective strength in order to have what it takes to change the world! **Baby Boomers, Gen X, Millennials and Gen Z, *together*!**

To bring this book to life, I have included real-life examples from the hundred-over interviews that I have conducted with education professionals, students, Human Resource (HR) practitioners, industry leaders and employees across all age groups. Their experiences and perspectives will be featured throughout the book and their names will be included, with their permission. In addition, between February and July 2020, I have surveyed more than 1000 people globally on their experience working with other age groups, and published the data in the *XYZ@Work 2020 Multigenerational Workforce Study*. Since their participation was anonymous, I have decided to bring them to life using Personas. The four portraits in Figure 1 below will be used to represent the respective generation that the quotes and the aggregate findings come from. So, even though the same four faces will be used throughout the book, the quotes come from hundreds of different respondents, across different parts of the world.

MEET THE 4 GENERATIONS
IN THE WORKPLACE

| Baby Boomer | Gen X | Millennial | Gen Z |
| 1946 - 1964 | 1965 - 1980 | 1981 - 1995 | 1996 - 2010 |

Note: These dates may vary slightly depending on geography.

Figure 1

Chapter 2

The Strategic Importance of Talent

In today's world one can hardly open a news site or read a business magazine without running into countless articles about *"The War for Talent"* or quotes by global leaders and CEOs talking about how employees are an organization's greatest asset. This is a significant shift in mindset that we are lucky to be witnessing. Only 30 years ago, when Baby Boomers dominated the workplace, an organization's market value mostly came from its tangible assets. Today, everyone knows that people are the ones who drive business success, and as a result Talent Attraction and Retention has become a critical business imperative.

The shift from a post-industrial to a knowledge society laid much of the infrastructure for the next major transformation of humankind. While machines will once again carry ample weight, in the face of Artificial Intelligence (AI), the humans who will design, operate, manage and work alongside these machines are of even greater importance. What values will they have? How will they navigate multicultural and multigenerational environments? What is good and what is fair in the digital age?

With technology taking prime stage, the need emerged for a different talent profile. T-shaped and polyhydric individuals, capable of dealing with complex systems and of moving swiftly between social and technical tasks became a necessity for most businesses, yet scarcely available. In the *2020 Outlook Study by Universum* 40 percent of CEOs admitted to being "unable" or "barely able" to hire the talent needed to meet their business goals. In the *2018 PwC Global CEO Survey*, 80 percent of CEOs expressed concern about the availability of key skills (a number that has been increasing year-on-year over the last decade), and cited the lack of key skills as the biggest threat to an organization's growth prospects — alongside cyber-attacks, populism, geopolitical uncertainty and social instability.

This goes to show that even prior to the Covid-19 Pandemic, most of the world's largest economies were underway to face a serious workforce crisis. With AI shifting the division of labor between humans, machines and algorithms; organizations and governments on a quest towards Automation, Robotization and Digitalization causing a global shortage of technology talent; rising start-ups pulling engineers out of traditional jobs; and the "gig economy" forcing companies to rethink the way people are employed, the talent landscape was already evolving at light speed.

The 2020 global crisis fast-tracked this disruption. Aside from destroying the livelihood of people all across the world and pushing their healthcare systems to the brink of collapse, the Covid-19 Pandemic has unleashed a worldwide economic pandemonium, and the impact on *The Future of Work* is greater than any of us can even imagine. Many industries — retail, travel, hospitality, oil and gas, financial services to name a few — have sustained lasting damage and will have to reinvent themselves in order to survive. Many of the jobs already at risk of becoming obsolete due to digitalization will be permanently wiped out, and hundreds of millions of workers will have no choice but to learn new skills and join new sectors. The precarity of the contingent workforce model has been exposed, requiring systemic changes that will likely accelerate its wide-spread adoption. The countless number of start-ups that went bust for lack of funding will push back into the market thousands of entrepreneurs, benefitting those organizations that are willing to drive change and innovation through corporate intrapreneurship or entrepreneurship programs.

As both business and political leaders all over the world struggle to anticipate and prepare for what is to come, one thing is certain: the Covid-19 Pandemic has elevated the strategic importance of talent even further. Not only will the future require a much more calculated, flexible and sensible approach to employing, recruiting, developing, re-skilling and up-skilling people; but the pivotal role in turning this humanitarian crisis into an opportunity will be played by the new generations working hand-in-hand with the older generations to chart a more positive trajectory and solve the many interconnected problems we will increasingly be facing. *"Global crises that crush existing orders and overturn long-held norms, especially extended, large-scale wars, can pave the way for new systems, structures, and values to emerge and take hold. Without such devastation to existing systems and practices, leaders and populations are generally resistant to major changes and to giving up some of their sovereignty to new organizations or rules."*

As Daniel Araya wrote in the Forbes article titled *The Revolution After the Crisis*, we are on the verge of a complete social renewal, and if it is true that every generation seeks to resolve the crisis of the last, Gen Z will be the catalysts for this *Second Global Renaissance*, one that will "replace market dogmas with digital humanism".

For organizations, being able to combine the drive, resilience and social mindedness of today's youth, with the broad range of skills and experience of senior employees will mean the difference between surviving and prospering.

Chapter 3

The Millennial Impact

One cannot talk about the need to harmonize the generations at work without fully understanding the impact that the Millennial Generation had, not only on the workplace, but on society as a whole. Most of you reading this book have likely been bombarded with literature on Millennials, guides on *"How to... all things Millennial"* and feel you have heard enough. But please bear with me: in order to look forward, it is imperative we take a step back and look at the changes this incredible generation has been able to bring about, changes that benefited all of us and that are now paving the way for Gen Z to achieve even more meaningful things.

Millennials forced the world to recognize one thing: ***young people matter***. They ***do*** have valuable and important things to say, they ***can*** and ***should*** contribute, they ***can*** achieve great things and build strong companies, and their voice ***should*** be heard. Let's pause for a second and realize how big this is. Prior to Millennials, the general consensus — in some parts of the world more than others — was that youngsters are like empty containers, they have a lot of space needing to be filled by people with experience, and only after being thoroughly indoctrinated by older generations or after developing enough expertise of their own, they would finally have something worth listening to.

As a Gen X, I myself have been a victim of this mindset, as have most people born before the 1980s. When I was 21, after graduating with high honors from a U.S. University, I decided to move back home to Italy and start the much-dreaded process of looking for a job. I was "lucky enough" to be hired by a large global advertising agency as a "Junior Account".

Needless to say, I was dismayed when I realized that instead of working with clients, participating in pitches and listening in to meetings, my duties consisted of making photocopies, typing emails dictated by my boss, cleaning and organizing the dusty archives (which were not digital back then) and going on endless coffee runs.

Furthermore, I learned that socializing during work hours was unacceptable and was cause for immediate termination. The photocopier machine was in the same small room as the coffee vending machine, so as I made copies, colleagues from other departments would often drop by to get themselves a drink. Naturally — in those fleeting moments it took for the coffee to come out of the machine and into the cup — we would exchange a few words. But one of us was always on high alert. If we heard footsteps in the corridor, we would abruptly end the conversation because if someone senior saw us talking we would be reminded — and *not* in a nice way — that **this was work!** We were not paid to chit-chat, and if we were caught doing so again there would be consequences.

One day, bored of my menial duties, I asked — no begged — my boss to allow me to quietly sit in on an internal meeting between the Accounts and the Creative teams. This "insubordination" resulted in me being called in by HR. I was told that I was too eager and too ambitious, that these requests were inappropriate and unacceptable, and that I needed to "stay in my place". But I did not let that stop me, I was young and full of drive and I wanted to prove it. So, I started a colossal project, a full-market analysis of an entire car segment (I was on the team working with a French automotive company). I worked on it relentlessly until late every night. When it was complete with all its graphs and charts and I felt proud of it, I brought it to my boss, telling her I worked on something — on my own time, of course — that I thought would be highly beneficial to the team. She picked up the bound report from my hands and started flipping through the pages. I could see in her eyes that she was impressed, and I started feeling hopeful. *She noticed me and would finally acknowledge my potential! My experience working for this agency was about to change!* Instead, she handed it back to me with a straight face and said, *"Next time, if you decide to work on something nobody has asked you to do, and give it your superior, make sure at least that the pages are properly aligned."* This because a couple of the 50-plus pages came out slightly angled from the printer, something most people would not even have noticed. Then I was dismissed. This was when I realized that no matter how much I tried, I was the "rookie", and nobody was going to listen or give me a chance to develop any expertise that would make me "worth listening to".

Before deciding to resign, I called my grandfather Piero. He was a Traditionalist and a hardworking guy. He was in his 80s and still going strong as a workplace lawyer in his own firm. I vented to him about how small I felt, how unappreciated and hopeless. I told him I studied hard, and graduated top of my class, so that I could go on to learn and do something with myself, and I felt I was being precluded of any opportunity to do either. When I was done, I waited hopefully for some words of encouragement or understanding. What he did instead is what triggered my profound love for Employer Branding, and subsequently Generations at Work, a few years later. Instead of being supportive, my grandfather scolded me! He asked me what was wrong with me! I had just started to work and had to keep my head low, pay my dues. I was lucky they were even paying me. *Lucky they are even paying me?!?* I thought. *Isn't that what work is all about?* I did not buy it, I resigned and moved on. I did experience similar unfortunate situations again; I even recall an instance where the CEO of one of the organizations I worked for refused to meet the new batch of interns during a company Christmas party because he saw them as *"nothing but a cost"*.

Eventually, I ran into three bosses — atypical for their time — at the three subsequent companies I joined, who recognized my potential, took a bet on me and gave me ample space to fly. What saddens me the most, looking back, is how many remarkable young people I encountered along my path who will never truly know their value and how much they could have achieved had they not been seen only as young inexperienced people who represented a cost to the company and little more. Of course, one thing I did not realize at the time, was that this was not unique to Italy, but was what many Gen X all around the world experienced upon entering the workforce, and that Baby Boomers and Traditionalists, like my grandfather, had it even worse.

To be honest, I often wonder how much more I would have been able to accomplish had I been born in a time or a place where a young person's ambition and vitality were rewarded and not suppressed. So, you will understand now why, despite being myself challenged by Millennials every single day, I have a profound sense of respect and gratitude for their generation, for what they represent, and for what they managed to accomplish by rising together and changing the status quo — as the Baby Boomers did decades before them (I will discuss this in more detail in Chapter 12).

Although initially criticized for promoting and encouraging reckless behavior, *YOLO* (the acronym for "You Only Live Once") that flooded the internet in 2011 and was originally intended as a "tip" for the older generations, ended up defining the Millennial approach to life and career. For one, Millennials decided it was time to put an end to the concept of work brought about by the Industrial Revolution. No longer should people be corporate slaves — working in cookie-cutter offices or cubicles, hiding their passions, molding their uniqueness and their individuality to suit everyone around them for the benefit of an employer that would not think twice about letting them go on a moment's notice the second they no longer fit in or performed the way they were expected to. No longer should people put their life on hold, spending most of it working in the hope of finally being able to do all the things they always dreamed of after retirement. *Life is now, it should be experienced now!* Because of their sheer numbers and the strength of their conviction they had to be heard, and they were able to send a message loud and clear: *work should be part of who I am, not just a way to make a living*!

But how did it come to this? Let's go back to the early 2000s — the Dotcom bubble burst, the 9/11 terrorist attack killed nearly 3,000 people, the War on Terror and the war in Iraq began. Big players like Parmalat, Enron and WorldCom collapsed after fraud investigations, and Al Gore's book *An Inconvenient Truth* started shedding light on the issue of Climate Change just as the world registered record-high temperatures and 400,000 people died because of natural calamities between the U.S.A. and the Indian Ocean. At the same time, Millennials watched their parents waste their entire lives at jobs that made them wither, work relentlessly day after day, mold into people who had little in common with who they were on their private time, be absentee parents and spouses, age without ever making a difference, and put aside any dream of experiencing the world until after they retired because the two-week vacation a year they were granted would not allow it.

Then 2008 happened. As the world economy collapsed and many of the banks were wiped out, millions of people in the U.S.A. alone who put their lives on hold to work and save their earnings for a better future lost their jobs, their homes and every penny they had put aside. ***Boom!*** A life gone by, dreams that could now never be fulfilled, and precious time with family that could never be reclaimed.

During that time, as I was working on a project for a large multinational company, I ran a focus group with college seniors. What one girl said has always stayed with me. She shared something personal and significant. She told me that she came from a traditional family — the mother stayed at home taking care of the kids and the household, while the father worked. He was in banking. The mother was an introvert and soft spoken, while the father was an extrovert with a good sense of humor. In the morning, during breakfast, the father would make jokes, sing and make the kids laugh. His energy filled the entire room. But when he came home late in the evening he was a different person, one she hardly recognized. He was depleted and the light he naturally carried was gone. Initially, she thought the long working day was to blame. *How could her dad not be exhausted after working for 12 hours straight*? But then she realized that her mother, who worked around the clock relentlessly taking care of the house and her siblings, was always herself. No matter how much she worked, her essence did not change. The girl realized the working hours were not the culprit, but the fact that the minute her father left the house he had to wear a mask and hide all those beautiful characteristics that made him unique, in order to fit the corporate environment of his employer. What ultimately changed him so drastically was the fact that he spent most of his life forcing himself to be different than who he really was. She decided that day — as would many other Millennials around the world — that she would only work for an employer that would allow her to be herself and feel "home at work", and that a friendly working environment and work–life balance were more important than prestige and a high salary.

Not only did people lose their jobs as a result of the financial crisis, but thousands of internships were rescinded in the U.S.A. alone (I am mentioning the U.S.A. because this is where Millennials first "appeared"). And as grave as the situation was, many Traditionalists and Baby Boomers saw a silver lining. Now that Millennials experienced hardship firsthand, they would be "knocked off their high horse", stop the nonsense and realize that it is much better to have a job — any job — than no job at all. Things would go back to the way they "*should be*". What happened instead is the complete opposite!

The year 2008 cemented Millennials' belief that life should be lived as it happens, and that one cannot spend an entire lifetime doing something they hate for people who do not fully appreciate them, when they could be spending time with their loved ones, doing things that make them happy. Instead of folding, they came together — disillusioned by the current status quo, yet hopeful about the future — and by doing so, they changed the rules of the game.

The Google Phenomenon

At the same time, **Google** happened. A company started by kids in a garage. A company claiming and showing that young people can make great things happen. That a work environment does not have to be sterile and lifeless. That people do not have to pretend to be someone they are not. That there is value in diversity. And that what makes people unique is an asset to be embraced and leveraged. Google advocated that employee well-being is important, and provided good quality food, massage and rooms for resting. Advocated that creativity is important, and built game rooms where employees could play, because after all play fosters creativity. Advocated that employees' personal life and affections are important, and started granting more personal days and even the ability for them to bring their pets to work. Advocated that people should be free to pursue their own passion projects, and launched *"20% Time"*, allowing employees to spend 20 percent of their time working on what they personally believed would benefit the organization. Furthermore, Google recognized technology as an enabler, and while many organizations were blocking or penalizing the use of social media in the workplace for fear it would kill productivity and encourage workplace gossip, the tech giant allowed — and even encouraged — employees to use social media sites while at work to share ideas, cooperate and solve problems. There it was. Out of the dust, a mirage! A company made up of young people, where young people's needs were met, and it was not just a startup: by then, it had the strength of an Initial Public Offering (IPO). How different from any other employer out there!

I still remember what work was like in 2006. I had recently joined a global Employer Branding company to build its Advisory team in the U.S.A.;

this was where I started helping employers better understand this new generation, define their Employer Value Proposition (EVP) and develop Employer Branding strategies to attract them. Six months into the job, the CEO asked me to join her for a meeting with one of the **Big Four Accounting Firms** in New York. We were at the final stages of pitching a large global EVP project that I would be leading. As I made my way towards the Philadelphia train station to catch the 7 a.m. Amtrak train to the City, I received a call reminding me of the five rules that had to be followed when visiting a client: light on the makeup, no cleavage, closed-toe shoes, no colored nails and possibly an updo hairstyle. Of course I had! This was the appropriate way to dress for a business meeting back then.

As a side note, I still advise the same company, and boy, how things have changed! We have meetings in "unconventional places", people dress informally, women's fingers often showcase colorful nail art, some have pink or purple highlights in their hair, and I have even been offered wine during a 3 p.m. — Wednesday meeting. Nothing else changed: the intellectual level of our discussions is still the same, the company is still going strong — if not stronger — and our encounters are as productive as they ever were, if not more. It is impossible not to notice how much happier people are when they are free to be themselves, and how much easier it is to come up with good strategy when you do not have the pressure to fit into a specific mold, but can bring who you truly are into the discussion.

It has now been more than a decade since Google first rose to the top of most-ideal-employer rankings around the world, and it is still in the lead. Companies often ask me why, considering many other organizations have followed in its footsteps and started offering a similar working culture. The answer is simple: Google will forever represent the Workplace Revolution. Google defines the Millennials in much the same way the Beatles defined the Baby Boomers back in the 60s. Millennials had a vision; Google had the answer. And this is how a new generation of youngsters and a tech company, hand-in-hand, forever changed the workplace as we knew it.

Chapter 5

Life Careerism

In the past, battles for talent were mostly won by the largest organizations, those with the strongest brands, leaders in their industry, who could promise rapid career advancement and good remuneration. Likewise, ideal candidates were chosen primarily based on academic achievements and work experience. When attracting graduates, the focus was on their school, their grade point average (GPA), and the companies they had interned with. Among high achievers, the international banks, the Big Four, the management consulting firms and the most popular multinational companies could take their pick, leaving local and smaller organizations with the option of either hiring tier two talent from tier one schools, or venture outside of the crème-de-la-crème in the hope of hiring the top talent from lower-ranked universities.

Those of us who graduated in the late 1990s or early 2000s will remember being encouraged to read career guides listing the questions employers were likely to ask during an interview, and exactly what we were expected to say. Success depended on our ability to memorize those answers and repeat them to the interviewer with confidence and conviction. We were also heavily discouraged from asking how many vacation days the company offered, as it would make us look "lazy". If we were asked to share one character flaw, the expected answer was *"I'm too hardworking."* Where we saw ourselves in ten years? *"Bringing maximum value to the organization, of course"* and so on. In short, companies would select a candidate based on his or her ability to mold into their corporate environment, with little concern about whether the environment would be a good fit to the candidate's personality and vice-versa.

Most of us will remember how rapidly we shut down our MySpace accounts (the largest social networking site in the world at the time) after organizations started firing people based on the personal information they shared online. Employees posting a photo where they were seen drinking at a party would fail to "uphold the image of their employer", hence had to be let go. Back then, we not only avoided talking about our personal lives and likes, we made a conscious effort to keep them concealed from our employer for fear of being judged or worse.

But not Millennials. They had no problem talking about themselves and did not fear sharing their personal lives on social media. After all, if an employer had a problem with a 20-something having a life outside of work and doing what 20-something people do, it meant it was not the right organization for them to be working for anyway. With Millennials — and now Gen Z — individuality took center stage. Millennials wanted to "feel home at work". With the newfound belief that they should be valued and respected for exactly who they are, Millennials started looking for companies based on good cultural fit and jobs that would match their personality.

Employers had to rapidly adapt. It was not long before they realized that in this new environment, academic skills and achievements were no longer the main selection criteria. That although two organizations belonged to the same industry, their ideal talent was likely to exhibit different traits. They started favoring candidates with international experience, humility, ability to culturally integrate and think outside the box over ones with high GPAs or graduating from top Universities. A student who spent an entire summer backpacking in a foreign country became a more appealing candidate than someone who took an internship at home. Suddenly, assessment criteria completely changed.

With the desire to feel home at work and the expectation that employers become catalysts to fulfil their bigger picture, new career archetypes started to emerge. Gen X (who viewed a job as "just a job") could be easily classified into three main career archetypes according to Universum research: Careerists — *who want to follow a promising career path in a prestigious environment*; Hunters — *mercenaries who chase lucrative and competitive jobs*; and Leaders — *who search for jobs where they can further develop their leadership skills*. With Millennials, however, Hunters started disappearing (big problem for companies that need to fill sales positions and are now forced to rethink these roles and how to attract people into them), Careerists became a shrinking pool, and Leaders remained as scarce as they ever were. Harmonizers — *who prefer a stable work environment characterized by a respectful and balanced management philosophy*; Idealists — *who are attracted by employers whose ethical and sustainable principles and values are in line with their own*; Entrepreneurs — *who seek an evolving environment where they can own and solve challenging problems*; and Internationalists — *who are open-minded and prefer to be internationally connected by meeting new people, traveling and working abroad* — became the fastest growing career types. Organizations realized that by talking solely about prestige and financial benefits they would continue to attract Careerists but would alienate Harmonizers and Idealists who are likely to represent the majority of the young generations going forward.

All of a sudden, recruiting became more and more like dating. Today, it is not about settling for a candidate exclusively based on their grades, educational attainments or experience, or choosing an employer based on the prestige of its brand, but about finding the best possible fit between the candidate's personality and the company's culture and environment. *"What's your personality type?"* is not a question you would have ever expected to hear in an interview as a Gen X or a Baby Boomer. However, with life and career merging, employers are now expected to support their employees in their aspirations beyond work. It is by understanding "Life Careerism" — the need to embrace the values and beliefs of each career archetype and what motivates job seekers on a deeper emotional level — that employers are able to differentiate themselves from their competitors and thereby build a sustainable advantage in talent acquisition.

Chapter 6

The Rise of Gen Z

It is now time to turn our attention towards the latest wave of talent. In a 2018 article, McKinsey named Gen Z *"True Gen"* because of their relentless search for the truth. *"Gen Zers value individual expression and avoid labels. They mobilize themselves for a variety of causes. They believe profoundly in the efficacy of dialogue to solve conflicts and improve the world. Finally, they make decisions and relate to institutions in a highly analytical and pragmatic way. That is why, for us, Gen Z is 'True Gen'."*

Technology plays a big part in their "search for truth". Gen Z are addicted to their mobile devices and rely on specialized online communities and influencers for information. Since their media use is on-demand, they often rely on secondary sources, and with algorithms determining the content they are exposed to, what informs their choices, actions and beliefs differs depending on the media they consume. *"It's hard to generalize about my own generation, Media fragmentation has played a large role in the diversification of our generation, so much so that two individuals living in the same area and attending the same school may grow to become completely different from each other due more or less to the media consumed by each,"* Isabella Williams, a Gen Z from Australia told me. This makes Gen Z even more difficult to attract, recruit, engage and retain.

Remember how Millennials caught most of us unprepared? Time to, once again, brace for impact because Gen Z will not be any easier — on the contrary, they will force organizations to transform once more, in more ways than one.

The Disruption of Higher Education

Gen Z will likely cause a decrease in the number of those pursuing traditional university degrees, warranting a significant transformation of both the educational system and organizations' recruiting practices. While previous generations prioritized graduate and post-graduate degrees, Gen Z prefer to do training within the workforce. According to *Universum 2015 Gen Z Study*, 72 percent of global Gen Z aged 15–19 would consider skipping college if employers offered adequate training instead.

This shift in perspective is amply justified. Because of Millennials' high demand for education, the cost of a degree skyrocketed, but being super educated did not translate into higher salaries. While higher education presumes higher productivity and hence higher earnings, in the 2000s productivity and compensation decoupled and most college graduates did not receive an increase in compensation proportional to their productivity increase. *"We fear there will be an increased workload, increased inflation rate, but a stagnated pay. In a society where tax rates are increasing, and the rate of growth of starting pay for fresh graduates is lower than inflation, we worry about our future. Imagine studying for the first 25 years of your life, only to receive basic pay, insufficient to sustain yourself, for the next 10 years,"* Lynette Lim Shuek Hwee, a Gen Z from Singapore told me.

In certain markets, particularly the U.S.A. and the U.K., student loans have become unsustainable, and many degrees do not accelerate earnings enough to offset the costs. As a result, long-term education became less appealing than jumping straight into a paying job. Furthermore, the prime argument for acquiring a degree — so you can launch your career in a higher salary bracket — does not appeal to Gen Z who value experience over tangible possessions and are not as driven by monetary rewards as the older generations. Concurrently, the growth of alternative education and online learning tools has further reduced the importance of a brand name school on a resume. In the past, in order to attend a lecture by an Ivy League professor, one would need to attend an Ivy League school.

Today, particularly in a post-Covid world, most lectures are made available online and accessible by all.

And then, there is *The Future of Work*. As industries converge, new jobs requiring a new set of skills will emerge. In "Jobs of Tomorrow: Mapping Opportunity in the New Economy", the *The World Economic Forum* identified seven emerging high-growth new professions that will account for 6.1 million new job opportunities between 2020–2022. This means the new generations will need to shift their focus entirely from academic skills to distinctive skills, including Business Skills, Specialized Industry Skills, General and Soft Skills, Tech Baseline Skills and Tech Disruptive Skills. Many of these are not currently taught in Universities, or at least not effectively, and many doubt the current educational systems will be able to transform quickly enough to meet the demands of the future workforce. In short, for education to be worth their money, it will need to ensure Gen Z gain skillsets that are in high demand: polyhydric, transferable and durable.

For the declining number of Gen Z who are considering a formal education, pure interest in the subject matter is now the primary driver when choosing the course of academic study. They want to dedicate their time to something they enjoy and that will make it possible for them to help others. While on the upside this means there will be greater focus on Humanities, Communications and Arts (which will be in demand as AI takes over more of the technical roles), it also means a steep decline in those pursuing STEM (Science, Technology, Engineering and Mathematics). *"One contributing factor may be that there is now a much wider variety of career options than there used to be. Jobs, today, are much more multi-disciplinary in nature and there is quite simply a much wider choice of what students can both study and work in after they graduate,"* Professor Anjam Khursheed, Director of the Engineering Science Programme, **National University of Singapore (NUS)**, told me. *"Educational institutions must introduce more combinations of subjects that can be taken with engineering. Changes to the curriculum need to be made so it will be easier to combine the study of engineering with other subjects, such as those in business, science and* *the humanities."* As part of a push towards broad-based education, and to allow for "greater flexibility and the cross-pollination of disciplines", in September 2019, NUS announced its plans to form College of Humanities and Sciences in 2021.

When it comes to technology, according to Gen Z, it should not be a separate course of study, but the common thread that cuts across all subjects and disciplines. They are worried that if educational institutions do not catch up quickly, they will not have the skills necessary to face the future. According to Michael Nugraha, a Gen Z from Indonesia, *"Gen Z's most significant concern regarding our future is having the many skills required for even simple jobs, as the job market will be getting more competitive. Since the world is getting more complex, interdisciplinary will be necessary because it's not anymore just about science or technology, it's science AND technology. It won't be just about ecology, or sociology, or anthropology. A more interdisciplinary approach will be demanded by society and employers to face the upcoming challenges."*

Like NUS, educational institutions around the world have risen up to the challenge and created cross disciplinary curricula with a strong real-life experience component in partnership with top organizations. **The Sandbox**, the innovation and entrepreneurship office of **Ngee Ann Polytechnic** in Singapore, for example, works with top organizations including **Visa**, **PayPal**, **OCBC**, **UOB**, **DBS**, **Standard Chartered Bank**, **Prudential** and **OneConnect** to develop initiatives and programs meant to nurture and deploy student's entrepreneurial spirit and provide hands-on training to develop critical skills.

The pace of change that educational institutions are experiencing has further been hastened by the onset of Covid-19. Institutes of higher learning have had to quickly find ways to move content online, keeping students engaged with home-based learning and ensuring they stay up-to-date with the skills required by the industry. And just as the Pandemic has accelerated a future where employees can work from anywhere, it will also redefine how and where students will pursue their education. *"What does the future hold for our students? I am sure is a question most educators are asking themselves. Our responsibility as educators is to instill in the students that education is a lifelong process. Students have to take a self-directed and proactive stance to upgrade themselves so they can continue to stay ahead of the curve, while adjusting to the fact that online learning with a mix of classroom learning is here to stay,"* Tan Ching Ching, Director of The Sandbox, Ngee Ann Polytechnic said.

Governments around the world are also becoming more invested. Singapore, once again leads the change. As it rapidly turns into a "Smart Nation", the government is addressing the growing demand for talent with skills fit for the future by redefining its approach to education. While historically Singapore educational institutions have been primarily focused on developing strong academic skills, from 2023 onwards the focus will no longer be on grades and exam results. Instead, children will be encouraged to create their own personal learning journey through personal development, discussions and applied learning skills. The City-State also aims to become the global leader in developing and deploying scalable impactful AI solutions in key sectors by 2030, and one of the key priorities covered in the national strategy on artificial intelligence, unveiled in November of 2019, is to ensure people have the necessary skills to work on and alongside new technologies. In order to accomplish this, Singapore has plans to train 25,000 professionals in basic AI coding and implementation by 2025.

So, when it comes to Gen Z and their view on education, whether the future will see a significant number of them walking straight from high school to the workforce will depend strongly on whether governments, organizations and universities will take this as an opportunity to transform. Aside from the growing number of Corporate Universities, there is a rise in hybrid programs with governments around the world facilitating partnerships between universities and organizations. In 2017, Dyson founded the **Dyson Institute of Engineering and Technology** — "an immersive engineering degree for the next generation" — in partnership with **University of Warwick** in the U.K.. The four-year program uses the degree–apprenticeship model of delivery, which combines an academic course of study and a work-based element of learning alongside Dyson's global engineering team. Students are paid a salary to work on live projects at Dyson whilst studying full-time, and the cherry on top is they graduate debt-free.

Finally, as can be expected, some of the most progressive organizations like **Google**, **Apple**, **IBM**, **Bank of America** and **Tesla** are already hiring talent without a University degree. Elon Musk is one of the strong advocates that it is not what you know that matters, not where or how you learned it. In a Twitter post dated February 2, 2020, he announced that **Tesla** is recruiting and that "*a Ph.D. is definitely not required... I don't care if you even graduated high school,*" as long as candidates have strong knowledge of AI and know how to code. In July of 2020, **Google** announced a new suite of *Google Career Certificates*, a selection of professional courses to help Americans get qualification in high-paying, high-growth jobs in six months, without the need for a college degree. Kent Walker, SVP of Global Affairs at Google, said in a Twitter post dated July 13, 2020, that the company "*will treat these new certificates as equivalent to a four-year degree for related roles.*"

While higher education will continue to be the main source of talent for the foreseeable future, one thing is for certain: employers will need to start considering how they will adapt, grow or establish their training and development programs to effectively engage the new generation and teach the necessary skills. They will also need to rethink how they collaborate with educational institutions, and their criteria when sourcing talent, i.e., is a prestigious college degree the most effective way to identify the best person for a job?

The Quest for Purpose

While it is true that our collective attention started shifting towards the environment with greater force with Millennials, it is also true that little has been done about it, and the consequences of climate change have since greatly deteriorated. After all, not only global leaders, corporations and governments have been slow to react, but much of the progress made over the last decade is now being reversed; the Trump Administration rolling back close to 100 environmental rules and regulations and the U.S.A. withdrawing from the Paris Agreement, Brazil pushing through with further deregulation of environmental policies, increasing deforestation and habitat destruction, and human overconsumption — just to name a few. And these are only the issues related to the environment; poverty, hunger, healthcare, social inequality, human rights and aging population complete the list, with the Covid-19 Pandemic exacerbating all of them.

At the World Economic Forum in Davos in 2019, Marco Lambertini, Director General **WWF International** advocated *"the need for an unprecedented cultural revolution in the way we connect with the planet,"* stressing that *"if we continue to produce, consume and power our lives the way we do right now, forests, oceans and weather systems will be overwhelmed and collapse."*

It is not hard to understand why Gen Z would feel a strong sense of urgency. Well-travelled and globally connected, they recognized early on that humanity is facing significant global issues and they feel a sense of responsibility to turn things around. Unlike their Millennial counterparts, who upon entering the workforce optimistically believed they could change the world by working for the private or public sectors, Gen Z have little trust that anything will be done without their direct contribution. They do not believe that Corporate Social Responsibility (CSR) or donating to charities is an indication of an organization's genuine interest or commitment to "do good" (more like a "tax deductible" with huge PR upsides), hence feel that in order to make the world a better place, they must take matters into their own hands. A study has shown that 55 percent of older Gen Z globally (as many as 88 percent in Indonesia) are interested in starting a business predominantly because they see it as the one sure way to drive significant **impact**. *"I want to start a company and design my own products because I see a lot of problems with the world. Society is hypocritical. We say we want to be eco-friendly, yet we use technological advances to produce and sell more products that will eventually be thrown away. I want to target hyper* *consumerism by creating new products modular in design and combining functions of existing ones, allowing for users to only need one such product (shoe, jacket, multi-functional chair) that is high quality and long-lasting. This is my life's mission,"* Daniel Foo Jun Wei, a Gen Z from Singapore told me.

This need for change is not limited to the entrepreneurs among Gen Z; even those who are considering corporate employment choose organizations that have purpose threaded within their DNA, and hold them accountable for bringing about the change they advocate. They also expect to be enabled by senior leaders to work on projects that deliver traceable impact, not only to the business, but to society as a whole. According to the *XYZ@Work 2020 Multigenerational Workforce Study*, 91 percent of Gen Z students say the ability to drive social impact is important when considering their future career or future employer. In particularly, they want to address issues surrounding *Inequality*, *Education*, *Poverty*, *Sustainability* and *Climate Change*.

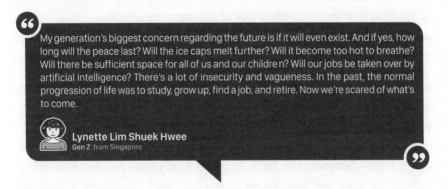

> " My generation's biggest concern regarding the future is if it will even exist. And if yes, how long will the peace last? Will the ice caps melt further? Will it become too hot to breathe? Will there be sufficient space for all of us and our children? Will our jobs be taken over by artificial intelligence? There's a lot of insecurity and vagueness. In the past, the normal progression of life was to study, grow up, find a job, and retire. Now we're scared of what's to come.
>
> **Lynette Lim Shuek Hwee**
> Gen Z from Singapore "

Figure 2

Chapter 7

Ethical Consumerism

As consumers, Gen Z are redefining consumer power, believing they can make a greater impact on the world through their buying choices than through the people they vote for. Their consumer behavior is motivated by ethical, environmental and political considerations. This philosophy has led to the term *"Buycotting"*, where individuals ensure their everyday consumer spending reflects their values. A 2019 study showed that up to three in four Gen Z are likely to buy products from a brand as a way to endorse an issue the brand supports; and likewise, many would stop supporting a brand that does not share their same values. With mobile commerce broadly adopted by this generation, exercising this choice has never been easier.

Much like Millennials with *"Work Environment and Culture"*, Gen Z will be driving the next big shift, and it will be related to *"Purpose and Impact"*. And for those who think the 2020 Global Crisis is going to make them backpedal, think again. I have heard the same thing over a decade ago. In much the same way the 2008 Financial Crisis strengthened Millennials' resolve to work for organizations that showed respect and empathy towards the individual, the Covid-19 Pandemic will further reinforce Gen Z's determination to engage with companies that not only have high ethical standards, but adopt environmental and social responsibility as part of their business model, and back it up. With Gen Z, greenwashing will simply not do.

The *"buycotting"* philosophy is redefining how companies advertise, as the past approach of branding a product as "Number One" in the market is no longer effective. The line between Employer Branding and Consumer Branding will blur, blend, and eventually disappear, as organizations realize that they can sell products more effectively by aligning the brand with a bigger mission, rather than using traditional consumer messages.

Corporate Citizenship will soon become a must for any organization looking to establish a strong Employer Brand. Not only because it is the right thing to do, but because on one hand, young consumer behavior is motivated predominantly by ethical, environmental and political considerations, and on the other, Gen Z — being strongly driven by impact — will only consider working for employers that have a strong, well-defined purpose and can enable them to contribute in a meaningful way. In short, with Gen Z, communicating Purpose will become the main competitive advantage for organizations looking to attract both consumers and future talent.

When it comes to having a clear purpose, few companies can outclass **Patagonia**, one of the world's top brands for outdoor clothing. The company is well-known for its unconventional workplace. When you visit the career section of their website, the first thing you see is a big picture of an employee working on his computer wearing swim shorts, resting legs and sandy bare feet on his desk. Owner and Founder Yvon Chouinard even set a policy, which he talks about in his memoire *"Let My People Go Surfing"*, encouraging employees to drop work as soon as the surf comes up to go enjoy the waves. But clothes and a friendly and flexible working environment is not all Patagonia is known for. Despite being a one-billion-dollar-a-year company, Patagonia has a clear mission statement, one that can be found at the front and center on their website: *"We're in business to save our planet."* And they are serious about it. Patagonia uses only high-quality organic and ethically sourced materials to make products built to last, and urges people to buy less. They launched *"Worn Wear"* with the goal of extending the life of their products and cutting down on consumption. Not only do they encourage the sale of used items, but they go as far as sending a camper van around the U.S.A. to repair customer's damaged clothes and equipment. This is just the tip of the iceberg. Activism is the second tab on their website; here they encourage their customers to get involved in the environmental cause they feel most passionate about by connecting them with action groups in their local community.

Patagonia is a great example of a company able to build a strong lucrative business while caring for its people and weaving love for the environment in its business model. To no surprise, the stronger Patagonia fights against consumerism and in favor of the planet, the more the brand sells, and the better talent it attracts.

More and more organizations have started to redefine their mission, and many have successfully managed to align purpose and profit through **Sustainable Profitability**. In June of 2020, **Unilever** has announced a One-billion-euro Climate and Nature fund to fight climate change, protect and regenerate nature and preserve resources for future generations by ending its contribution to deforestation, promoting regenerative agriculture, protecting water resources, making its products biodegradable, and reaching net zero emissions by 2039. In its annual update on sustainability programs, released in June 2020, **Amazon** also announced its commitment towards the environment. The Climate Pledge Fund will further accelerate investments in innovations for the low-carbon economy of the future with an initial two billion dollars funding for companies with solutions and products that will facilitate its transition. Amazon also confirmed it intends to run on 100 percent renewable energy by 2025, five years earlier than previously planned, invest in nature-based solutions and reforestation projects around the world, and reduce packaging waste.

Sadly, unlike Patagonia, Unilever and Amazon, the majority of organizations cannot "walk the talk", and even those associated with robust social and environmental programs are unable to link them back to their business or their vision for the future. As a result, according to a recent Gallup study, 60 percent of Millennials do not feel connected to their company mission, a number likely to rise with Gen Z.

Chapter 8

The Important Role of Today's Youth

The Covid-19 Pandemic will not only strengthen Gen Z's resolve to contribute to something meaningful, but will surely leave a long-lasting impact. Much like the Great Depression for the Traditionalists, the end of World War II for Baby Boomers, the Fall of the Berlin Wall and the Dotcom Crash for Gen X, and the 9/11 terrorist attacks in the U.S.A. and the 2008 Financial Meltdown for Millennials, the year 2020 when the world went on lockdown — and its aftermath — will likely represent the defining moment of this generation.

Let's look at how the Covid-19 Pandemic disrupted their education and their debut into the workforce. From one day to the next, they were no longer allowed to go to school and had to attend lessons and take their exams through digital platforms. The graduating cohorts were not able to collect their diploma on a stage and celebrate their accomplishments surrounded by their friends and family; and with campus recruitment on halt, many missed the opportunity to meet with employers and understand more about the different career options available to them. Finally, the lucky ones who secured an internship or a job that were not rescinded, had to onboard and begin their assignment virtually, without any in-person interaction, through programs rushed to market. While the less fortunate were told their offers had been withdrawn and found themselves yet to find employment.

Even before the Covid-19 Pandemic, young people were struggling to adapt to a rapidly changing society, mostly because the current education system is still overly focused on the acquisition of knowledge, and not enough on preparing them for *The Future of Work*. *"My generation suffers from depression, anxiety, stress, and inferiority. Young people are afraid of not being a prodigy, fearful of not excelling, anxious of being vulnerable, stressed because of social norms, depressed because they are constantly pushed and are not being heard by those who should've listened, feeling inferior to others because they seem to have their life figured out,"* Michael Nugraha a Gen Z from Indonesia told me. *"We live in a world where the job market demands high skills, there are high expectations on what we accomplished in school, when in reality we didn't even have the time to figure out what we wanted or what we excelled at because of high demands. The education system asked us to be a prodigy, to excel at everything, to be the impossible, to all be equally perfect, but in reality we are just humans each with our different interests and skills."*

The economic impacts of Covid-19 will fall heavily on young people, especially those working — or planning to work — in the most affected sectors, like retail, travel and hospitality, where hiring reduced significantly. In this new climate, leaders will have two important roles going forward: look beyond their own talent needs and help young people across every country become productive and engaged members of society by equipping them with the necessary skills; and give their own Gen Z employees a voice, helping them become the great leaders of tomorrow. *"The current events, from pandemics to environmental catastrophes, have led to a resounding pessimistic approach towards the future. I hope this can re-invigorate my generation with a heightened sense of their place in the world, and instill faith in pro-active and sustainable change environmentally, politically or culturally,"* Isabella Williams, a Gen Z from Australia told me.

Their drive and desire to change the world, combined with the adaptability, resilience and humanity that Gen Z will inevitably form as a result of the hardship they endured, are exactly what society craves. The Public and Private Sectors are increasingly finding ways to collaborate with Non-Governmental Organizations (NGOs). The younger generations are seen as activists, taking positive actions and driving change; as conscious consumers, expecting positive change from organizations with sustainable practices; and as future talent, holding many of the skills required to drive businesses into the future.

Agrim Singh, a Millennial Engineer from India whom I spoke with, thinks both the world and the workforce can greatly benefit from the arrival of Gen Z. *"It will be great having them join the workforce. They are sharp, mission-driven, risk-averse, speak their mind and harness the power of the collective instead of trying to change the world alone. Gen Z is a big champion for diversity which means better talent in a workplace. Given technology and ease of access to personal development, Gen Z are likely to have talents, areas of knowledge and broad interests beyond their college majors. What matters to Gen Z beyond anything else is working towards a big mission and knowing that their employer aligns themselves to something meaningful. Projects like 'it is what it is', which leveraged FOMO (Fear of Missing Out) and Twitter to get people to raise money for Black Lives Matter charities is one of many such examples,"* he said.

A company that has been very successful at putting the above strategy into action, is **Unilever**. Apart from its commitment towards sustainable business practices, the company has been putting more and more emphasis on developing and launching "Youth Initiatives" aimed at building youth employability and responsible citizenship through free and easily accessible learning. In 2016, Unilever launched a work readiness program in South Africa called **Level Up** to help address the issue of youth employability and equip young talent and future leaders with future-fit skills for the modern workplace. Level Up has been designed to democratize opportunities, empowering Africa's youth and boosting them into sustainable careers through monthly masterclasses, free certifications, and nine specialized modules they can complete in their own time. These include: Finding your purpose, Choosing your path, Exploring the right jobs, Building your Brand, Applying for your chosen job, Interview skills, Onboarding, Career counselling, and Diversity and Inclusion. *"Youth have incredible potential. They are creative, tenacious and ambitious. We just need to believe in them and create space and opportunities for them* *to thrive. Level Up as a workplace readiness program is a step in the right direction to level-up the playing field and to accelerate the rate at which we develop young Africans with the knowledge and skills to lead in corporate, in government, in NGOs and as entrepreneurs. Helping youth get ready for their career journey is the responsibility of every corporate citizen,"* Mechell Chetty, HR Vice President South Africa, Unilever told me.

As One Young World founder Kate Robertson said in a number of interviews, supporting young people on the ground is particularly important because they are connected and familiar with the needs of their community and therefore more likely to find the right way to address them. **One Young World** identifies, connects and promotes young leaders giving them a global platform, and partners with governments and educational institutions to empower young peace builders around the world. Furthermore, through **Lead2030**, One Young World funds and accelerates Sustainable Development Goals created by founders under 30. In May of 2020 One Young World partnered with the Bill and Melinda Gates Foundation and United Way to provide funding to youth-originated projects around the world that directly tackle community needs arising from the Covid-19 Pandemic. To get a glimpse of how committed youth is today one can look no further than the *One Young World Summit* — also known as "Young Davos" — where thousands of leaders and young people come together every year to address and find solutions to the world's most important issues.

"My hope is to see the brilliant young leaders we work with today emerge in positions of power. Where they are really calling the shots. I look at the young people we work with around the world and I just imagine that they will become the leaders of the G20, then they can lay me down and carry me away because then my work is done. Because once they are there leading companies and governments the world will be a better place! I have to believe that, it's not advice, but certainly a call to action," Kate said during a 2018 interview.

Another great example is **The Kairos Society**, a global community of young entrepreneurs, top students, and global leaders who aim to solve the world's greatest challenges. Each year young talent from around the world gather at the *Kairos Global Summit*, where influential CEOs, mentors, startups and young entrepreneurs share their vision of the future and start potential collaborations with these young talents. During the Kairos Global Summit, the list of the 50 most promising companies worldwide with a founder or cofounder under the age of 25 that addresses a global challenge is announced. The Kairos Society is supported by international mentors like Peter Diamandis, Richard Branson, Bill Gates and Bill Clinton.

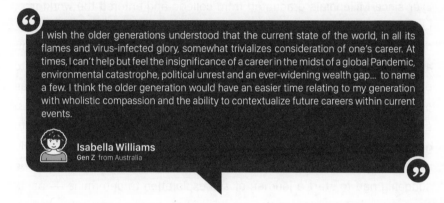

> I wish the older generations understood that the current state of the world, in all its flames and virus-infected glory, somewhat trivializes consideration of one's career. At times, I can't help but feel the insignificance of a career in the midst of a global Pandemic, environmental catastrophe, political unrest and an ever-widening wealth gap... to name a few. I think the older generation would have an easier time relating to my generation with wholistic compassion and the ability to contextualize future careers within current events.

Isabella Williams
Gen Z from Australia

Figure 3

Chapter 9

A Limited Window of Opportunity

Ever since Millennials graduated from college and entered the workforce, I have helped hundreds of employers understand, attract, engage, coach, develop and retain them. Nobody expected Millennials to be so different, and when they started flooding the workforce, organizations began to panic, particularly traditional industries like banking, professional services or financial services. How could they compete with Google? In the past a strong brand, good benefits and leaderships opportunities were enough to get first pick. But now that things had changed, how could they possibly attract a generation so selective about the work environment? Companies suddenly had to start a journey of self-exploration to determine — aside from their performance in the stock market, or the popularity of their products — who they were, what they stood for, what they wanted to become, where they needed to change, and what they could offer talent in terms of development, environment, experience, and values. After answering these questions, they were ready to bring to life their newly unveiled EVP with incredible stories of happy employees, working flexibly with friendly people on meaningful projects. These messages were delivered to perspective talent — first on campus or through recruiters, and subsequently through digital channels — and to employees, as a way to strengthen engagement and retention. You may remember the early EVP Taglines: **Hewlett-Packard**'s *"Be Yourself Be an Inventor"*, **Johnson & Johnson**'s *"Be Vital"*, **General Electric**'s *"Imagination at Work"* or **Microsoft**'s *"Come As You Are, Do What You Love"*. This was the beginning of Employer Branding as we know it.

Fifteen years later, organizations are still struggling with the changes brought by the Millennial generation, but few of them truly have their eyes set on Gen Z. I find this surprising, and somewhat puzzling. For years, I heard HR executives and business leaders discuss how challenging adapting to Millennials has been, how they wish they had been able to anticipate the changes Millennials brought about and claim first mover's advantage. Gen Z are now on their doorstep, yet, organizations are foregoing the golden opportunity to connect with them early. What leaders and HR professionals need to understand is that by the time Gen Z are ready to enter the workforce, they will have already been guided and influenced.

On the recruitment front, the main challenge for employers will be finding talent with the required competencies. We have seen in Chapter 6 how the scarcity of engineering talent will become even more evident, and how all industries will become recruitment competitors. In short, there will not be enough Gen Z technical talent for everybody. Employers will have to play their cards right; ensure they are top-of-mind and position themselves as top employers. This will require a clear vision, a strong purpose and a culture that enables and empowers Gen Z to make significant contributions within a short period of time.

Big promises, however, are not enough. Organizations will have to ensure their workplace, **and everyone in it**, is ready and willing to embrace Gen Z. Companies need to deliver on "the promise" by bringing to life what is communicated in the recruitment process across every career life stage. Teddy Yang, a Millennial and experienced HR professional at **Procter & Gamble**, believes the key to retaining young talent lies in the manifestation of an organization's EVP. *"If an employer promises young talent coming through the door that they will drive innovation and make an impact, it needs to make sure it delivers this experience through meaningful job scope, ability to share creative perspectives and influence decisions, and supportive line leaders who encourage this to materialize, instead of having bureaucracy get in the way."*

This means there needs to be genuine commitment from the entire organization to welcome, guide, listen, and empower them.

With four generations in the workplace, this is not easy. Baby Boomers and Gen X often do not understand how to engage Millennials and Gen Z, why they need to spend so much time coaching them, or even why they require (and should be granted) so much flexibility. In most cases, this is no fault of their own: the reality for a young individual entering an organization today is polarly opposite from what it was back in the 1980s or 1990s. It is then to be expected that those who do not have a natural curiosity and knack for people may be unaware of what the new generations crave, what they respond to, what they need in order to feel engaged, and what they expect from their manager. When this happens, companies that attract talent with the promise of leaders who will inspire and empower them will fail to retain them, despite their best efforts. Intergenerational conflicts are a big reason why young talent leaves an employer, and for many organizations this is a growing problem. It is hard enough to attract the right people, but not being able to keep them is extremely costly, without counting the amount of time invested in training talent who will then take what they have learned straight to a competitor.

The reality is that while most organizations are desperately seeking innovative and purpose-driven individuals, few provide an environment that would appeal to the typical Gen Z. In order to prevent them from being disappointed and leaving shortly after they join, it is extremely important that employers ensure there is **cross-generational awareness within the existing workforce**. If Millennials taught us one thing, it is that any employer who fails to quickly adapt and embrace positive and meaningful change will surely be left behind!

Chapter 10

The Rise of Generational Diversity

With Baby Boomers delaying retirement, Gen X ready for succession, Millennials reaching leadership positions, and Gen Z new to the workforce, organizations must learn how to create the best possible environment for a vastly diverse group of people. Unfortunately, as the demographic shifts vary across the world, a one-size-fits-all approach does not work. In some countries, like Japan or Italy, the older age groups still make up the majority of the workforce, and the very old will double over the next 60 years. In other countries, like Vietnam and India, the younger generations dominate. This diversity of age and experience has created a cultural divide exacerbated by young employees often supervising older, more experienced ones.

Diversity can be a great asset to a company, introducing fresh perspectives and applied knowledge. However, when not handled with care, it can create a volatile environment, which leads to obstacles in communication and conflicting expectations. Baby Boomers, Gen X, Millennials and Gen Z have different modi operandi and when these are not recognized, productivity and customer satisfaction get derailed. Optimal performance relies on strong communication across all levels of the organization and a clear understanding of everyone's role. Employees of all generations want to feel recognized and respected for their contribution; they want to know that their career path has a clear trajectory and they want to be able to perform their job while still enjoying time with family and pursuing personal goals.

The problem lies in the shifting definitions of key words such as **"communication"**, **"respect"** and **"flexibility"** across the different generations. What seems reasonable and desirable to one generation can seem inappropriate or even unfair to another. This results in having different age groups distracted from their work by a seething sense of mutual resentment.

The generational disparities within a company can also leak out to affect interaction between the business and its clients. Let us consider the challenge of a Multi-National Corporation (MNC) trying to appeal to a younger customer, if their work team is predominantly from the older age group, or vice versa. In order to attract the widest possible customer range, companies need a diversity of voices and viewpoints within their ranks. When a team is not working in unity, overall customer service will suffer as it will be difficult to delegate tasks, develop creative solutions or solve problems effectively in an atmosphere of conflict and misunderstanding. So, it is in the company's best interest to examine the challenges of an intergenerational workplace and find proactive solutions.

Some industries have understood the value of fresh perspectives way before the Millennial Workplace Revolution. Fast Moving Consumer Goods (FMCG) is a great example because of its need to constantly win over the next generation of consumers. During a conversation with Rene Co, Baby Boomer and Vice-President, Communications and Sustainability at **Procter & Gamble**, Greater China, he shared his experience joining P&G in a marketing role in 1992 while fresh out of University. He still remembers his first day at work because of something his new boss said: *"You studied marketing and communications so you learned about the Product Life-Cycle Model, everything that rises will eventually decline. Well, we don't believe it! Your job will be to build brands that pass the test of time. The key to achieve this is to always find a way to remain relevant and attract younger users."* Of course, nobody understands young consumers better than young consumers themselves. This is why over the years more and more organizations have made it a priority to hire the brightest talent straight out of University and provide them with the best training. This ensures a steady stream of young people who, while lacking in experience, can bring fresh perspectives.

At the same time, Baby Boomers continue to be incredibly important. Sadly, because they are on their way to retirement, they might not be an organization's top priority when it comes to professional development or career advancement. However, they possess a wide range of invaluable skills, and their many years of service guarantee a wealth of knowledge and experience that the younger generations simply cannot beat. Organizations have a lot to gain from retaining Baby Boomers and providing them with opportunities for upskilling and reskilling in an environment where they feel comfortable, appreciated and valued. After all, they are not just responsible for the transfer of institutional knowledge, they are also the ones who need to guide young generations to leadership.

Shortly before writing this book, I was having a chat with Stephen Tjoa, a Baby Boomer and Partner at **KPMG** in Singapore. Stephen shared with me his memories of being a young Baby Boomer fresh out of school, as well as his view on challenges and opportunities they face in the Multigenerational Workforce today. *"Late phase Boomers and Gen X like me have seen a lot in their lives. We saw how simple life was before, but at the same time, we witnessed enormous technological progression that quickly transformed the way we did things. Given our exposure to the various cycles and at least half a dozen crisis situations, we learned quickly to adapt, change, and stay resilient. Our experience is invaluable when it comes to providing historical and institutional learning. I believe many of our experiences will have weight when we look at how things may succeed or fail. As we have spent most of our lives connecting with others at a more personal level, we have more well-defined relational skills than the generations that came after us. Relating at a personal level is a fundamental skill, particularly now that significant amount of communication has gone virtual as a result of the Covid-19 crisis,"* he said. *"Older generations were taught to express themselves effectively through speech and writing and to develop strong interpersonal relationships. From what I see today this is a lost art yet much needed if we truly want to be catalysts of change."*

Furthermore, the tables are now turning. Millennials are no longer the youngest generation in the workplace, Gen Z are arriving in staggering numbers and Millennials often doubt their ability to manage them. At the same time, sandwiched between generations (as Gen X were before them), many are experiencing the *"Middle Child Syndrome"*, struggling to define themselves, needing to mediate to get everyone on the same page, and having to be both students and teachers. *"As the 'in-between generation' we have the pressure to learn whatever we can quickly from Boomers and Gen X, be patient and show respect. At the same time, we are expected to teach Gen Z and allow them to contribute with their own skills and mindset, so they can feel good and create value in hierarchical structures as well,"* a Millennial from the U.S.A. said.

Understanding Generational Diversity is particularly important for family-owned businesses. The difference in mindsets between First-Generation owners and their heirs, the parents' concern that their children may not be ready to take over, and the frustration of the Next Generation that feels unable to innovate the business, frequently lead to family disputes and succession issues. I will talk more about how family-owned businesses can address these challenges in Chapter 28.

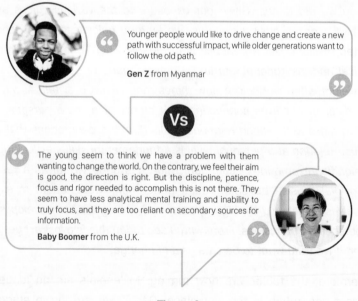

Younger people would like to drive change and create a new path with successful impact, while older generations want to follow the old path.

Gen Z from Myanmar

Vs

The young seem to think we have a problem with them wanting to change the world. On the contrary, we feel their aim is good, the direction is right. But the discipline, patience, focus and rigor needed to accomplish this is not there. They seem to have less analytical mental training and inability to truly focus, and they are too reliant on secondary sources for information.

Baby Boomer from the U.K.

Figure 4

PART 2

The Multigenerational Workforce — From Baby Boomers to Gen Z

"Each generation imagines itself to be more intelligent than the one that went before it, and wiser than the one that comes after it."

George Orwell

Chapter 11

The Truth Behind
Intergenerational Conflicts

While most organizations understand the importance of embracing Generational Diversity, differences still lead to discord among workers, low employee engagement and stagnated innovation. According to the *XYZ@Work 2020 Multigenerational Workforce Study*, only 59 percent of Baby Boomers, 66 percent of Gen X, 43 percent of Millennials and 40 percent of Gen Z believe that having four generations makes the workplace more productive, and two-thirds of respondents find it hard to work with colleagues from other age groups. The cause is mostly rooted in **different mindsets**, **hierarchy**, **technology** and **communication,** leading to a series of underlying conflicts that hinder not only an employer's ability to retain talent, but the opportunity to leverage on each generations' unique strengths to drive workplace happiness and productivity. Generational diversity of human capital will lead to even greater challenges in the coming years unless organizations are able to address it by being more open, innovative and adaptable.

In the many years I have helped organizations understand the main cause of attrition, one thing became clear: people most often leave their employer either because of lack of professional advancement, or because of intergenerational clashes. Poor communication combined with conflicting expectations can be a source of tension between generations. When Baby Boomers entered the workforce, it was common for people to stick with their first job for life, climbing the corporate ladder in-house. Baby Boomers were motivated by the "big picture" and they defined prestige and success in terms of salary and career advancement.

REASONS FOR INTERGENERATIONAL
CONFLICTS IN THE WORKPLACE

Work ethics, attitudes and career perspectives are tremendously different between generations: so are reference points, motivations and the base emotional level. Attitude towards authority, timeliness, consumption are at variance. The differences are so innate and deeply rooted that leaders across each generation usually find them rather unsolvable in reality. Precious resources are wasted in unnecessary and needless friction.

The problem lies in communication: the workforce is less productive simply because we still don't know how to communicate effectively with one another and optimize our generational strengths. If we find a way, and employers help us, there is so much potential. Right now there are too many reservations and conflicts that create a ridge between people who should be working together, so there is little trust. When there is no synergy and lack of empathy, you are bound to see more conflicts.

It can be chaotic. A lot of ego clashes. Experience vs risk-taking. Clashes in values make it difficult for new ideas to turn into action, especially since older cohorts have more institutional power to quash innovation. It is also harder to form a consensus and build a culture across varied backgrounds and experiences. Seniority often kicks in together with generational differences exacerbating generational divides and reducing social cohesion. Cultural shifts are also harder to internalize due to conservative mindset and diverse opinions.

There is a significant difference between 'old school' and 'new age' thinking. Old generations are stuck in their ways and are reluctant to change. We want to progress quickly but are unable to grow because our speed and input are undervalued. This leads to frustrations on both sides. Boomers and Gen X see us as impatient and naïve and think we don't respect their experience, and we see them as close-minded, rigid and unappreciative of our energy and desire to drive positive change.

Figure 5

Confined to a nine-to-five workday, they would work overtime to prove their loyalty, and defer personal enrichment experiences — such as travel — for retirement. Gen X followed this pattern, except that they did not stick to the same company. They advanced by changing jobs whenever a better opportunity presented itself, seeking prestige not just through their title but through their association with big-name brands. Millennials and Gen Z have a different approach to their career. Due to technological advances, they take flexible working conditions for granted, and work on their own terms to create an enriching work–life balance. Rather than prestige, they are motivated by a sense of purpose and want to work in an organization where they can achieve something bigger than their own personal goals.

For Baby Boomers and Gen X, promotion and higher compensation were the reward for working hard. *You work, you get paid. You demonstrate leadership and loyalty, you get promoted.* In contrast, Millennials and Gen Z are fairly distrustful of a company culture based on dominance and prestige hierarchy. They are paid volunteers, more interested in a supportive and creative environment that provides flexibility to pursue their personal interests. Yet, they want more individual acknowledgement than any previous generation. Feedback is a top issue in intergenerational dynamics. Older generations only expected feedback when something was done wrong (or *exceptionally* well), hence they do not give the continuous reaffirmations that the younger generations need.

Having grown up with constant access to the Internet and the ability to do anything from anywhere, Millennials and Gen Z feel constricted by the type of work environment that the older generations considered the norm. Meanwhile, as digital skills become more important, senior employees are at a disadvantage to younger, tech-savvy workmates, and feel left out from tech-enabled conversations. Some companies have over-corrected by banning the use of social media platforms during work time, leaving younger generations feeling frustrated and voiceless. As an added source of tension, younger generations tend to reject authority and structure, and frequently bypass the chain of command in order to meet their own goals. This makes their managers and leaders often feel disrespected.

One of the biggest frustrations comes from the desire of Millennials and Gen Z to explore new ways of thinking, working, and addressing problems. Baby Boomers and Gen X are seen as more resistant to change, with a tendency to rely mostly on their past experiences. *"The biggest conflicts in the workplace today come from the fact that older generations often have an established view of ways to accomplish tasks, and are reluctant to try new things. Younger generations, on the other hand, want to do things differently right away, but don't necessarily have the knowledge, experience and maturity to navigate uncharted water,"* a Gen X from Hong Kong said.

You can see how mutual distrust is building up here. Baby Boomers and Gen X have patiently put in long hours, and they are close to reaching executive leadership positions or the rewards of retirement. But along come these youngsters whom they feel do not respect the patience and hard work that it has taken them to reach their position, and expect rapid promotion and a direct line of communication to top management. Millennials and Gen Z do not feel respected either, because they find senior employees unwilling to listen and acknowledge them for a job well done. The result is a dysfunctional workplace, where employees from all generations feel frustrated, voiceless and underappreciated.

The set views and opinions that generations have about each other is what leads to these assumptions. We see the same thing happening with people from different countries and cultures. According to Dr. Robyn E Wilson, this is a case of **Confirmation Bias**, seeing and hearing only confirming evidence. *"If a younger boss is struggling with how senior employees are working on a particular project, the story he/she will tell him/herself is 'they don't want to change because they will be retiring soon.' This prevents him/her from seeing and exploring alternative perspectives and to listen to* *others for the purpose of understanding (and not just replying). Frustrations abound and the young boss may never know how much the older worker can flex and change!"*

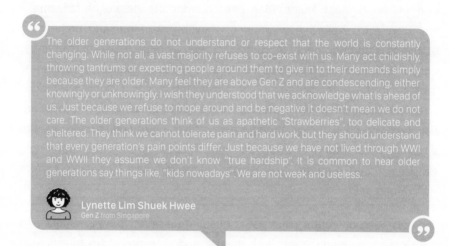

> The older generations do not understand or respect that the world is constantly changing. While not all, a vast majority refuses to co-exist with us. Many act childishly, throwing tantrums or expecting people around them to give in to their demands simply because they are older. Many feel they are above Gen Z and are condescending, either knowingly or unknowingly. I wish they understood that we acknowledge what is ahead of us. Just because we refuse to mope around and be negative it doesn't mean we do not care. The older generations think of us as apathetic "Strawberries", too delicate and sheltered. They think we cannot tolerate pain and hard work, but they should understand that every generation's pain points differ. Just because we have not lived through WWI and WWII they assume we don't know "true hardship". It is common to hear older generations say things like, "kids nowadays". We are not weak and useless.

Lynette Lim Shuek Hwee
Gen Z from Singapore

Figure 6

Chapter 12

Are Baby Boomers and Millennials Really That Different?

"A 60-something graduate recently reflected. We wanted what they want. We just felt we couldn't ask. Herein lies the truth: what young workers want isn't so different from what everyone else wants. However, young workers are asking for it."

— **Karen Cates and Kimia Rahimi**

Intergenerational diatribes are most common between Baby Boomers and Millennials. Their different views on leadership, office norms, and work–life balance can trigger tensions, creating obstacles in communication and blocking the transfer of institutional knowledge. Fifty-three percent of Millennials said they find it most difficult to communicate and collaborate with Baby Boomers. *"It's difficult to discuss issues with them when they have a different view: they always claim they know everything and are too controlling, but often they don't understand the current situation and yet refuse to adapt,"* a Millennial from Australia said. Likewise, 37 percent of Baby Boomers find it most difficult to communicate and collaborate with Millennials. *"They have unrealistic expectations of what they should get, a strong sense of entitlement. They are much more concerned about what a company can do for them than what they can do for the company,"* a Baby Boomer from the U.S.A. said.

I find this surprising for a number of reasons. Firstly, because Baby Boomers are often the parents of the very Millennials they struggle with in the workplace. They are the ones who taught them to follow their dreams, demand respect and work for someone who can unleash their potential. Every time I talk about this, I remember the beautiful scene in the 2006 American drama *The Pursuit of Happiness*, when Chris Gardner, played by Will Smith, tells his son, *"Hey, don't ever let somebody tell you you can't do something. Not even me, alright? You got a dream? You gotta protect it! People can't do something themselves they wanna tell you you can't do it. You want something, go get it! Period."* Yet, when Millennials approach their future work with this mentality, they are accused of being naïve, entitled, unrealistic, spoiled — even irresponsible.

Secondly, and more importantly, Baby Boomers and Millennials have a lot in common. Millennials are not the only ones to commend for driving The Workplace Revolution; Baby Boomers are the ones who started it. They are the generation who rose together against the "be seen and not heard" approach of the Silent Generation and decided to change the status quo. Baby Boomers were the original "Me Generation", often labeled *narcissist*s because of their desire for self-actualization. They were both the product and the beneficiaries of economic prosperity and in their quest for self-fulfillment, they became social activists, counter culturalists and political idealists. From the Sexual Revolution and the Feminist and Anti-War movements, to the Civil Rights and the Collapse of Communism in Europe, Baby Boomers created an era of freedom by either embracing or spearheading social change. Millennials are also not the first to be environmentally conscious, Baby Boomers celebrated the first Earth Day in 1970 and rose up in the thousands to volunteer after U.S.A. President John F. Kennedy established the Peace Corps in the 1960s.

In the workplace, Baby Boomers wanted to be heard, they wanted to break free from the "Control and Command" leadership style of older generations, but times were different and in order to accomplish this they had to play by the rules. They were Careerists by definition but Idealists at heart, and saw their rise to the top as the means to bring about change. If you think about it, you will realize that Baby Boomers worked hard and fought for many of the changes that the Millennials — thanks to their sheer number and the unique global context in which they arrived — were able to bring about. And yet these same changes are at the very heart of the conflicts between the two.

Do you think the Suffragettes — who fought relentlessly for decades to achieve female voting rights without ever casting a ballot — would resent women today for being an item on that very ballot? Would they see them as entitled because of the social status they enjoy and their desire for more? Or would they celebrate what they have been able to accomplish together — albeit generations apart? While this is something we will never have an answer to, I do know this: what the Baby Boomers started, the Millennials carried forward, and together these two generations paved the way for Gen Z to bring about even more change. Change that we are all going to benefit from.

Although seeing the younger generations have it "easy" can undoubtedly elicit bitter feelings, *"the Boomer generation, that pushed tolerance and diversity in the 60s, will also be required to stretch its own tolerance limits in order to accept young co-workers with new ideas about what is acceptable in the workplace"*. Likewise, Millennials will have to recognize the weight that Baby Boomers have pulled over the last half a century, what they have accomplished, and the fact that they set the stage for much of what the younger generations are benefitting from today. *"Current generations don't understand the advantages, rights and opportunities they have due to the contributions Boomers have made in challenging the status quo. They don't seem to know that the 1960s were a time of revolutionary change in human rights and rights in the workplace, as a result they have no respect for the hard work we put in to make these things happen,"* a Baby Boomer from the U.S.A. said.

As a Baby Boomer, father of four, manager and recruiting professional, I've had a great deal of direct experience with Millennials. Today's young people definitely look at the world differently than we did at the same age. Boomers went to college, got married, had children (in their 20s) and worked hard at fairly traditional jobs, simply because they were expected to do that. Most of us didn't question it. Today, it is more likely that young professionals will postpone getting married (if at all) and having kids until their 30s. Young people today spend far more time considering how they want to live their lives and where they will work and they are far more likely to start their own business. Generally, I think this is healthy; challenging the status quo is productive and spending more time contemplating how one lives their life is time well spent. But at times, the younger generations are not decisive and spend too much time considering their situation. Of course, thanks to the internet they have far more information available to them than we ever had. In the end, I think the greatest difference is Boomers are generally more conventional and Millennials don't feel bound by tradition or social norms. This includes less of a focus on wealth and the traditional accumulation of "things". But both groups seem to share a focus on quality of life, family, environmental responsibility and social responsibility.

Kent Kirch
Baby Boomer from the U.S.A.

As a Millennial working and interacting with older generations every day, I think Baby Boomers are highly valuable and bring a wealth of experience to the table, but the best leaders from that generation find a way to marry their experience with how the world has evolved in the time since they started working. Some of the thought process can be dated (for example, being anti-technology and not embracing it for work isn't a badge of honor given that there's an entire generation growing up with technology not as a luxury but as a necessity). There's a 'resistance' to accepting new ideas or ways things are done, especially if they veer from status quo. This applies broadly to how our generation lives their lives, with comments assuming our generation is immature and that there are only a finite number of ways to succeed professionally or personally (doing only certain degrees, only certain vocations are valuable). Something I wish they understood is that our generation isn't more sensitive than theirs (and stopped calling us a Strawberry/Snowflake Generation); Millennials are taking a concerted effort to talk about previously taboo topics like mental health/sexuality to deal with it better and not live a life of self-pity.

Agrim Singh
Millennial from India

The older generations think that we have become unbothered by the big questions of life and the standardization of what life should be (grow, study, get marriage, get a job in one industry, work, retire, die). I also do not think that they can keep up with the changes in the world and what has become acceptable. The world has changed with the advent of technology, the abundance of information, as well as new ideologies, like being multi-disciplinary in different fields, stronger support for entrepreneurism, taking up freelancing (YouTube/influencers), learning through online courses, skill share and equipping events/workshops. I hope Baby Boomers and Gen X can understand that life shouldn't be about going through the motions and becoming cyclical, but being adventurous and seeking experiences is more important than having a stable and sustainable job, settling down and having children. I think they should be more accepting of us having a stronger approach to life-long learning, constant excitement in life, and wanting to constantly evolve.

Daniel Foo Jun Wei
Gen Z from Singapore

Figure 7

Chapter 13

Let's Talk About Stereotypes

Any netizen has surely been exposed to passive-aggressive memes aimed at both Millennials and Baby Boomers. *"A Millennial who accepts constructive criticism? Now there's something I don't see often." "Raises the next generation by spoiling them. Says generation is entitled." "Oh, you're a Baby Boomer? Please tell me more about how terrible my generation is." "Says nothing in life is free. Wants to pay you in experience."*

In 2019, *"Ok Boomer"* has become a viral slang phrase used to dismiss out-of-touch or close-minded opinions associated with the Baby Boomer generation *and older people more generally.* Baby Boomers countered by accusing young people of making assumptions about them based on age, and not taking the time to engage before forming an opinion. *"I find 'Ok Boomer' to be a simplistic way to say 'I disagree and don't want to consider others' points of view',"* a Baby Boomer from the U.S.A. said.

While according to a 2019 New York Times article, *"'Ok Boomer' marks the end of friendly generational relations,"* I believe it represents a unique opportunity to finally address the elephant in the room, take a step back, and look with fresh eyes at one another so we can rewire, reframe and contextualize some of the behaviors, perceptions and biases that have prevented us from truly bonding.

The problem does not lie in the fact that other generations have traits, expectations and belief systems that differ from our own, but in the stigma attached to those idiosyncrasies. If instead of defending ourselves from what we see as unjust categorizations, we are able to accept that some may be true and justified — yet, do not negatively define us! — we can stop thinking of our distinctive traits as irrevocably discordant and start seeing them as complementary. In order to do this, we need to take an honest look — without judgement — at both our own generation and the way we truly feel about generations beyond our own. We need to put all stereotypes on the table and ask ourselves if they are really just stereotypes after all. Are the many internet-memes so far-fetched, or do they merely address frequently observed attitudes of different generations and the overall sentiment towards them?

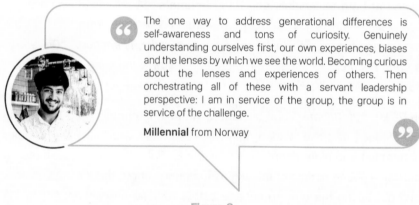

> The one way to address generational differences is self-awareness and tons of curiosity. Genuinely understanding ourselves first, our own experiences, biases and the lenses by which we see the world. Becoming curious about the lenses and experiences of others. Then orchestrating all of these with a servant leadership perspective: I am in service of the group, the group is in service of the challenge.
>
> **Millennial** from Norway

Figure 8

During the workshops I run for organizations to help bridge the generational divide, I conduct an anonymous survey to find out what is the most challenging characteristic that participants experience when working with each generation (including their own). When their aggregate responses are made available for all to see, I map them to the "stereotype". Here participants discover that the attributes they listed match the "stereotype" *every time.*

This is important for two reasons: firstly, those who are dubious and defensive can see that these are real and genuine experiences. Secondly, once the challenges people face with every generation are publicly revealed, participants can finally let the guard down, laugh with each other, open up, and embrace new perspectives.

Let's try this right now. Write down the top three most challenging characteristics you experience when working with each of the four generations below.

MOST CHALLENGING CHARACTERISTICS
OF EACH GENERATION

Baby Boomer

Gen X

Millennial

Gen Z

Figure 9

Now use Figure 10 to see how many of the characteristics are aligned — or closely aligned — with the general consensus.

MOST CHALLENGING
CHARACTERISTICS
OF EACH GENERATION

Baby Boomer	Gen X	Millennial	Gen Z
Hierarchical	Demanding	Detached from Work	Inexperienced
Stubborn	Individualistic	Over-confident	Impatient
Disrespectful of the Young	Pragmatic	Sensitive	Easily Bored
Conservative	Know-it-all	Entitled	Lack Focus
Resistant To Change	Insensitive	Insubordinate	Too Dependent on Other's Opinions
Risk Adverse	Distrustful	Disrespectful	Don't Know Hardship
Unempathetic	Skeptical	Unreliable	Addicted to Technology

Figure 10

Next, write down the top three strengths of each of the four generations, based on your experience working with them.

THE GREATEST STRENGTHS
I SEE IN EACH GENERATION

Baby Boomer

_____
_____
_____
_____

Gen X

_____
_____
_____
_____

Millennial

_____
_____
_____
_____

Gen Z

_____
_____
_____
_____

Figure 11

Use Figure 12 to see how many of your answers are aligned — or closely aligned — with the general consensus.

THE GREATEST STRENGTHS OF
EACH GENERATION

Baby Boomer	Gen X	Millennial	Gen Z
✔ Loyal	✔ Adaptable	✔ Creative	✔ Idealists
✔ Experienced	✔ Industrious	✔ Innovative	✔ Digital Natives
✔ Knowledgeable	✔ Independent	✔ Tech-savvy	✔ Environmentally Conscious
✔ Dependable	✔ Resourceful	✔ Enthusiastic	✔ Impact Driven
✔ Hardworking	✔ Sensible	✔ Open-minded	✔ Committed
✔ Wise	✔ Problem Solver	✔ Social-minded	✔ Fast Learners

Figure 12

Inevitably, there will be a number of you who did not like this exercise and who will agree with the quote below.

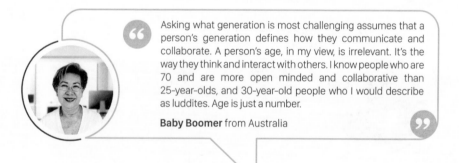

> Asking what generation is most challenging assumes that a person's generation defines how they communicate and collaborate. A person's age, in my view, is irrelevant. It's the way they think and interact with others. I know people who are 70 and are more open minded and collaborative than 25-year-olds, and 30-year-old people who I would describe as luddites. Age is just a number.
>
> **Baby Boomer** from Australia

Figure 13

However, **stereotypes are important**. They represent behavioral archetypes that cluster people together. This does not mean that stereotypes apply indiscriminately or that all people fit within a stereotype fully, but that statistically, on average, individuals belonging to the same group exhibit certain similarities. Stereotypes apply everywhere we look. In advertising we use behavioral customer models to target messaging. In digital product management we use user archetypes to design targeted user journeys. In sociology we segment social groups to inform policy. All of these could be called "stereotyping".

Every one of us has the tendency to self-identify with a particular "cluster" based on the people we spend time with, the slang (informal language) we use, how we dress, the media channels we follow, and the type of content we consume. It is natural for these preferences and behaviors to be somewhat influenced by the events that our generational cohort has witnessed and experienced. In a way, generations are sub-cultures, and then, naturally, they divide themselves in sub-sub-cultures. Saying that there is no generational divide would be like saying context does not matter. The context of each generation shapes its way of processing information, its values, its coping mechanisms, its parental style, its hopes and fears, and more.

It is true that in many ways we are all the same, and also — we are all different. But at the right level, some of us are more similar to one another than others, and generations are one way to group us together. In the words of Star Trek commander Lorca, *"Universal laws are for lackeys, context is for kings."*

Hence, openly acknowledging a stereotype — instead of becoming overly defensive — can benefit both sides. I may be oversimplifying it, but let me try to illustrate this with a personal anecdote. I was born in Italy, and despite living between the U.S.A. and Asia for more than half of my life, I consider myself an Italian through and through. As such, many of my personality traits are very aligned with the stereotype surrounding Italians.

I am loud and opinionated, I overtly use my hands in conversation, I get heated up when I am discussing something that I feel passionate about or I am trying to defend a position, and my reactions can sometimes be seen as "overtly dramatic" or "emotional". While I am not a big fan of the image of the Italian guy in Speedos, with a broken English, playing the mandolin on a Gondola, or eating meatball spaghetti, I must admit that the broader stereotype isn't that far off. Furthermore, it has, in some situations, played to my advantage. For example, it helped de-escalate potential conflicts and lead to greater understanding in my relationships with non-Italian friends and my Bulgarian husband. Being able to peg certain behaviors to a cultural stereotype, has helped others realize that they should not take it too seriously or too personally when I express myself in an overly passionate way, or that my waving my hands around is not a sign of aggression. It made me feel accepted, understood, and safe to know that I could be myself, and others would not immediately assume the worse, understanding instead that my reaction is a result of my cultural upbringing. At the same time, the stereotype made me aware of how others perceive some of the behaviors that most Italians would consider acceptable, handing me the choice to "tone down" my demeanor and be more sensible in the way I communicate dissent. So, although having been raised in a particular way should *never* justify being unkind or disrespectful to others, people are more likely to give you a free pass if they know that your behavior is rooted in your cultural background, and that it is not a reflection of your opinion of them.

In short: pondering on how they generally come across to others, instead of becoming defensive, can do wonders in helping both older and younger generations become more lenient, understanding and nonjudgmental, but also more self-aware, considerate and sensible in the way they interact with each other.

REASONS FOR INTERGENERATIONAL
CONFLICTS IN THE WORKPLACE

Baby Boomers shy away from ideas that go beyond what they are used to, are power centric, brag about experiences that are not applicable in modern days, have patronizing attitudes and are inflexible. They lack transformational thinking and refuse to learn and grow.

Gen X are driven by self-interest, have no loyalty to their work, are competitive, individualistic, cynical, and are not team players. They are not as adaptable to change, have a lot of preconceived notions and are set in their ways.

Millennials hold Boomers in contempt for leaving them a messy world. They have bought into the notion of a charitable, perfect, all-inclusive world with little idea how to support it. They harbor angst, are distracted, reject and experiential input. Google is nearly God.

Gen Z want everything without earning it, have no patience, lack a sense of hierarchy and are superficial. They want work to only come with pleasure. They do not know how to respect and interact with others, are self-centered and unwilling to accept other's opinions.

Figure 14

The Evolution of the Workplace From 1970s to 2020s

Although some historians dispute the legitimacy of the advertisement in Figure 15, I find that it triggers a great reality check for many of us today. For much of the 20th century this is what work was about. Forget the appealing Employer Branding messages we are bombarded

Figure 15

with nowadays. Forget the promise of thriving careers where we can fulfill our life's purpose, grow professionally, be supported by inspiring leaders, work from anywhere, pursue our interests and watch our kids grow. It seems impossible today that anybody would have ever answered such an advertisement. But whether this one is real or not, there were surely plenty like it, and people would indeed line up with hopes of getting the job. Think about the millions of immigrants who arrived in America by boat in search of a better future, or the hardships people faced in Asia and Europe following The Great Depression and World War I. For men with large families to support — sometimes a dozen kids — a job like this, even if it could cost them their lives (in mines and factories) was the one chance they had to ensure that one or two of their kids could go to school and have a better future. Throughout history, for most people around the world (and for many, unfortunately, still today) work was a necessity. It was something they were not expected to like or could be choosy about, but something they needed to do and were considered lucky to have. Selecting an employer based on whether it would match their personality, have a cafeteria and a pantry with free food, or would allow them to take their pet to work, was something no Baby Boomer or Gen X thought would ever be an option.

Obviously going back to the 1900s is taking it a step too far, but a glimpse into what work was like when the existing generations entered the workforce — and reflecting on how it has evolved from the time of Baby Boomers to Gen Z today — is a necessary step to understand the origin of certain behaviors, attitudes and expectations that are common among those who belong to the same generation.

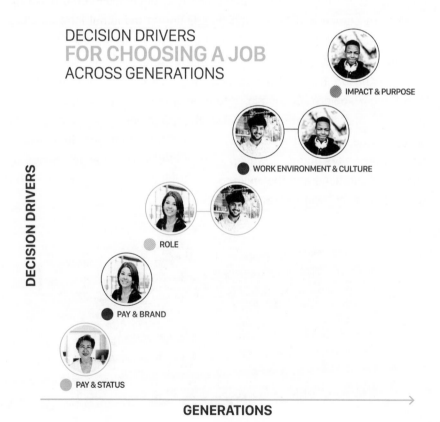

Figure 16

A Day in the Life of a Young Baby Boomer

"We were dizzy with our aspirations. We'd be rock stars. We'd be spiritual avatars. We'd be social activists. We'd be billionaires. No, better yet, we'd be all those things at the same time."

— P.J. O'Rourke
AARP The Magazine

When we talk about Baby Boomers, we typically refer to those born between 1946 to 1964. As discussed earlier, generations are defined by large-scale events. Baby Boomers in the U.S.A. were a product of the post-World War II industrial recovery and grew up in a period of unprecedented prosperity. In Western Europe and Japan, the destruction of industrial infrastructure delayed recovery by a decade. In India, the government-controlled economy affected economic growth until the 1990s, and in China, the political havoc of the *Great Leap Forward* and the *Cultural Revolution* only ended with Deng Xiaoping's Economic Reform in 1978. For these reasons, the timeframe and circumstances in which Baby Boomers (and subsequently Gen X) came to be, differed vastly between North America, Europe and Asia. What unites them, however, is their desire to "change" things in society, institutions and the "military industrial complex" (a term used by U.S.A. President Dwight D. Eisenhower).

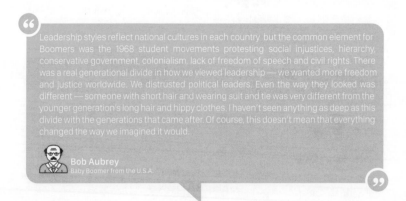

66
Leadership styles reflect national cultures in each country but the common element for Boomers was the 1968 student movements protesting social injustices, hierarchy, conservative government, colonialism, lack of freedom of speech and civil rights. There was a real generational divide in how we viewed leadership — we wanted more freedom and justice worldwide. We distrusted political leaders. Even the way they looked was different — someone with short hair and wearing suit and tie was very different from the younger generation's long hair and hippy clothes. I haven't seen anything as deep as this divide with the generations that came after. Of course, this doesn't mean that everything changed the way we imagined it would.

Bob Aubrey
Baby Boomer from the U.S.A.
99

Figure 17

When I think of Baby Boomers at work, one of the first things that comes to mind is a scene from *That '70s Show*, an American television period sitcom focusing on the lives of six teenage friends between 1976 and 1979. Particularly an episode where Eric, the main teenage character, decides to get a job after school to make some money. The job is tedious and his manager treats him unkindly to say the least, so he goes to his father Red Foreman, a retired factory worker and war veteran, to share his discontent. Much like how my grandfather reacted when I complained about my first job out of school (they were both Silent Generation, after all), Red gets mad at Eric and says *"Work is Work. It's not about fun, it's about seeing how much crap you can take from the boss man, and then taking some more."* In another occasion he says *"If it wasn't work, they wouldn't call it work! They'd call it 'super-wonderful-crazy-fun-time'!"* I think this pretty much sums it up. Work was *not* supposed to be enjoyable; it was something people had to do in order to live, gain financial independence, support a family, or earn wealth and status.

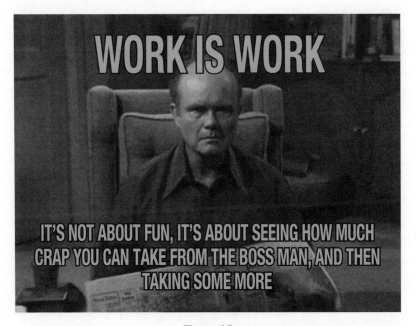

Figure 18

When Baby Boomers entered the workplace, the environment was conservative and quiet, and employees were bound by a strict code of conduct. The 1960s saw the rise of the cubicle, where staff worked in a tight space with rows of desks divided by partitions. It was thought that this type of set up — which resembled a factory floor — would increase productivity by ensuring everyone was visible. While staff sat in cubicles on the interior area of the office with no windows, senior employees had offices along the outer walls, and executives sat in large corner offices with many windows, representing prestige and power. *"We all wanted our personal space — a desk, a computer and partitions which gave us privacy. There was always a belief in necessary segregation as it was neater that way and one could focus. Office was office, home was home, work was work, personal was personal. I grew up thinking everything needed structure, fixed starting and ending times, and one had to work a lot of overtime to prove one's worth and dedication. The more voluminous your work, the more productive and diligent you were,"* Stephen, a Baby Boomer and Partner at **KPMG** Singapore said to me. *"The idea of work–life balance was folklore, and anyone taking flexible working arrangements was either lazy or lacking ambition. Progression, promotions and competition were things we talked about a lot among peers. We obeyed the rules, performed as well as we could and tried to move up as rapidly as possible. Structure and discipline were fundamental if we wanted to progress. Ultimately, we were all striving for that fully enclosed office space with a view and a personal secretary."*

Junior employees were expected to mostly listen, and entry level employees would not typically try to speak unless they were specifically asked for their views — which was rare — or had something extremely important to add to the discussion. In countries where most professional employment was "at will", everyone was aware that they could lose their job at any time for pretty much any reason, so young talent lived in constant fear of making a mistake.

A leader's job was measured by the ability to impart orders and increase productivity for the team. Employees, especially young ones, were supposed to follow the rules, do what they were told without question and show respect. Failing to adhere to these standards was considered insubordination. *"In my generation, there was a general culture of reverence for older and more experienced people. It was the culture at home and at school — 'do what you're told'. At the start of my career I stayed clear of any active open discussions that may have either led to disagreement, tension or discomfort. Whatever the boss wanted, I followed. Of course, it led to occasional resentment, but I always believed back then that this was the norm and I had to accept it until the day I would be a manager myself,"* Stephen continued.

Bosses had high expectations of performance, and there was a set of criteria that employees had to satisfy in order to progress. While there was an emphasis on continuous learning, the bulk of exposure was through direct working experience, and particularly through testing of an employee's capability in various situations. Leadership Development was not formalized. The most effective opportunity for development was having a strong boss who could share their knowledge, provide direct feedback and make sure employees focused on the right things.

Leaders were almost exclusively men and the *"old boy network"* attitude was as common in Asia and Europe as it was in the U.S.A. There was always a sense that one needed to be accepted in the "in-group", professionally and socially, because those who did would more likely be "helped" along the way.

Baby Boomers knew that they would have to "pay their dues" before getting to a rewarding position. Entry-level jobs consisted of many mundane activities; making photocopies, doing basic research, ordering supplies, or converting "manual" work into spreadsheets to make the process more efficient. There was no expectation that the tasks would be meaningful, interesting or challenging in the first few years. *"The use of spreadsheets was just coming into play when I started out,"* Kent Kirch, Baby Boomer and Former Global Director of Talent Acquisition and Mobility at **Deloitte**, told me. *"Being able to take budget and other information, quickly put it in a spreadsheet and calculate key stats in a short time, enhanced the value*

I was able to provide. I could do in about four hours what used to take someone over three days to do with a $100M dollar budget report. The office leadership (who was not PC literate) was astounded."

Tenure was incredibly important at the time, and job-hopping would hurt one's career prospects. This is the reason why many Baby Boomers had only a couple of jobs in their entire career. Their credo was to work at something as intensively as they could and never let occasional setbacks derail one's career progression or ambition. *"I always worked 60+ hour weeks during my entire career. I wasn't asked to do that, but I wanted to do the best job I could and I wanted to be known as a high performer. Many Boomers did what I did and some did much more. As a generation, we were strongly dedicated to our career success. But we also drove equality for women, work–life balance, environmental responsibility, and social responsibility. Many of these issues took root in the early 90s. In my view, the progress on equality for women in the workplace was a major accomplishment for Boomers,"* Kent continued.

Finally, starting a business was not nearly as popular then as it is today, and was often discouraged. The recommended path was always one with least resistance and less risk. When Baby Boomers thought about their education, it was always about choosing a course of study that would directly impact employability. Interests were secondary aspects that could only be considered at a later stage, once they reached very senior positions. The key motivators when choosing an employer were pay, benefits and stability.

A Day in the Life of a Young Gen X

Gen X is sandwiched between Baby Boomers and Millennials. Born between 1965 and 1980 in the West, and approximately until 1985 in Asia, Gen X, who rebelled against Baby Boomers' idealism, is considered politically non-ideological. *"Some would also argue that it is not merely the idealism of the 1960s that Generation Xers reject, but a deeper cynicism of the fact that such 'idealism', inevitably doomed in its gratuitous naïveté, so quickly gave way to an era unequivocally focused on commercial and industrial progress; a period which incubated many of the problems facing their and coming generations."* Bill, a Gen X from the U.S.A. agrees, *"Many Boomers sold out. They said they'd change the world, but in the end, succumbed to the base trait of avarice. Acquisition instead of building or innovating. Research and development considered an 'expense'. Nepotism. Shareholder returns as the priority. Outsourcing. Monopolies. Price-gouging. Wondering why they receive no loyalty from younger generations. They are blind to their avarice and hypocrisy"*, he said.

As the original founders of digital start-ups including Google, Apple and YouTube, Gen X is the first generation to have casual access to a personal computer. I still remember playing *Where In Europe is Carmen Sandiego* on a Macintosh 512K at the computer lab at school in 1984, journaling on my Pegasus computer at home in 1986, proudly carrying around my Apple Powerbook 5300 with eight megabytes of RAM in 1995, and patiently waiting for my dial-up modem to log me into my AOL mailbox (the most popular web portal and online service provider at the time) in 1996. So, despite not being "digital natives", Gen X are very comfortable with technology.

When early Gen X first entered the workplace at the end of the 1980s, most of the world was in deep recession and inflation was through the roof. Finding well-paying work was considered a luxury, and because a job was seen as "just a job", money was the key motivator. When the economy picked up in the 1990s, the concept of **Brand** took centerstage. *"The idea was to get the best pay and best title possible upon graduation, with little consideration for future career progression and the boss' leadership capabilities and compatibilities. Brand was also another big consideration, even before pay and title in some cases. A typical role we would aspire to would be a Junior Manager position, without necessarily a team to manage, but other responsibilities and exposure opportunities,"* Veronique Augier, a French-Indonesian Gen X, told me.

When looking for a job, even without previous experience, Gen X was expected to display the needed skills and the right attitude. They were taught to always look confident and not show any sign of weakness. Even asking how to perform a duty could make them look bad in the eyes of the boss, who usually expected them to "figure it out". As a result, they did not feel as strongly about professional training as their successors: needing to be trained could almost be seen as an indication that one did not have what was required. This negative attitude towards "being taught" was partly due to the fact that formal training was rare and limited to few organizations. Graduate schemes started to emerge towards the tail end of their generation, and mentorship and coaching were a notion and an advantage most Gen X could never have fathomed. Training usually consisted of having exposure to leaders for role-modelling. In short, whatever Gen X learned typically came from their boss. *"My boss would call me and three other colleagues into his office for 60 minutes every morning before the start of the regular work-day. The man had 40 years of industry experience and quite simply, opened his brain and imparted all of his knowledge onto us,"* Bill shared with me.

Because Gen X was expected to hit the ground running, not much time was given for induction, and buddy systems were uncommon. HR's role was admin, policies and procedures, and pay. *"There was no visibility of a career path, and accessing a leadership role was almost unimaginable. We were taught and prepared to start from the bottom of the ranks and to learn on the field. Induction was kept to a minimum; one day, if lucky, but usually just a half-day to do a tour and meet the teams, make introductions and present the policies and procedures. In my case, as a welcome present from my predecessor, I was left with a pile of five years' worth of files and no luxury of a handover. What made matters worse was my forerunner was portrayed as a superstar, so I had big shoes to fill with zero guidance or experience. Left to my own device, I had to learn on the ground, the hard way... and fast!!"* Veronique continued.

Bosses were strict authority figures. *"My first boss after graduation was an older man and super old-school. I had to shave, no facial hair allowed, not even a goatee. Suit and tie at all times, no business casual. If you were not in your seat by 8 a.m., the office door would be locked and you would not be allowed in until 9 a.m. We were vastly different from a generation standpoint. I believed in computers, he didn't. We had no computers, no Internet. Just phones and a red Dalton's directory and whatever newspaper classifieds you brought in to scope out jobs and employers. I was 'The Kid'. He was 'The Old Man'. When stuff got tough, he'd be ready to save the day. He was good and knew everything! He taught me everything over the course of five years, repeated it time and time again. While on the surface it was boring and repetitive, it drilled the best practices into my brain. So much so that I became the teacher later on,"* Bill, who started his career as a recruiter, explained to me.

Bosses had more experience, more credibility, more status and they made sure young employees were reminded of it with almost every interaction. Veronique told me she often felt uncomfortable around her manager. *"There was a lot of intimidation from my 30-something female boss who was very career-driven, who put her work before her family. She was hiding the fact that she was over four months pregnant with her second child, and was 'complaining' that her toddler barely recognized her. She expected everyone to stay in the office as late as she did. I was thoroughly micro-managed, made to feel untrustworthy. I was sent to Spain a few weeks after starting the job, alone, having to account for every single minute of that trip. My manager made sure my agenda was jam-packed with clients and partner meetings, barely any breaks and just enough time to go from one appointment to another, using only public transportation, in a country I'd never been to and in a foreign language I barely knew. Every single evening, from the hotel room, I was required to make a recap of my day via a phone call with my boss."*

The day-to-day duties consisted of menial tasks, repeated time and time again. Work was highly stressful, never knowing if what was put in would reap some sort of reward, or even be noticed. Whenever they got a more interesting assignment, Gen X felt they owed their boss for taking "a gamble" on them, especially if they had no previous industry experience or book of business. *"I felt my inexperience gave my bosses and older colleagues an opportunity to take advantage of me. I remember a lot of fear, it almost felt like I belonged to them and I owed them for being where I was. And of course, we were to treat management with extreme deference,"* Sarina Nel, a Gen X from South Africa, told me.

The office set-up was similar to that of the Baby Boomers, usually open and cramped up for most employees, with private offices for Senior Management. *"As a young hire, we would inherit whichever desk was occupied by our predecessor, but more often, the desk nobody else wanted. When another newbie came along, you would get a chance to pick second best dibs. I remember almost having to bring my own pens and stationery,"* Sarina explained.

Socializing during work was not allowed or encouraged, although relationships would naturally form outside of work. Instead of the comradery and "let's all rise together" attitude of Baby Boomers and subsequently Millennials, Gen X had to constantly fend off rivalry from colleagues. The work environment was cut-throat. There was a lot of internal competition for the boss' favour or a promotion. Leaders often encouraged and took advantage of it by pitting employees against each other to make them work harder.

When I was 22, I remember being told by a more experienced colleague that when you are a high performer and you think the reward is within reach, bosses often take away your spotlight and openly shine it on someone else with similar potential. *"Like jockeys do in horse races,"* I remember him saying, as if it were yesterday. *"They put blinkers to cover their horses' eyes throughout the race so they don't get distracted. As the winning horse leaves other horses behind and gets closer to the finish line, it becomes 'comfortable' so it tends to slow down. To get it to make better time, the jockey lets the horse slow down just enough to allow for the 2nd runner-up horse to get close. As soon as it is in the line of sight, the jockey quickly removes the blinkers on his horse so he can see the competitor advance. This makes the horse sprint and run even faster to ensure he reaches first."*

As you can imagine, this made Gen X always weary about others. At the same time, ironically, they were expected to work as a team, which meant working directly with colleagues who were after their job. *"The office environment was typically open so everyone could hear your phone calls. They would hear what you were saying, what you were working on. Sometimes colleagues would offer advice or intel on a subject, other times they played the role of 'shark' and tried to 'steal' your job orders or recruits. You always had to watch your back,"* Bill said.

This is one of the first lessons I learned from my father upon graduation. "**Never** befriend **anyone** at work! Everyone is a competitor! Never let your guard down with your boss! **Every** interaction, even in what appears to be a social context, even if it seems genuine, is an interview. Whatever you do, whatever you say beyond the professional, will **always** come back and bite you. Remember, you are just a resource, a number. At the end of the day it's business, and when you are no longer useful, no alleged 'friendship' will stop them from kicking you to the curb," he would say.

The code of conduct was Business Professional. Gen X was expected to look the part, play the part and act the part. The smallest details overlooked could cost someone their job. They were expected to uphold the same professional standard even in their private life (I mentioned earlier how many Gen X were fired in the mid-2000s because of what they posted about themselves on MySpace). *"As I grew successful, I became a bit 'unruly', staying out late, arriving late to work, sometimes with the hand-stamp from the night before still on. My boss would turn an eye, BUT, when it was obvious that things were slipping, he scared me straight, giving me a choice to either grow up or be gone. Money changes people. He brought me back to basics. Did not let me implode on myself. With regards to behavior, it was a professional office, so you had to behave as such, ALWAYS! There was fear of losing the job EVERY single day,"* Bill shared with me.

Finally, while many Gen X were under the influence of their Baby Boomer-parents who expected them to stay with the same company their entire career, most ended up rebelling and leaving to pursue prestige, higher pay or better leadership opportunities. To be promoted, they would often have to wait as many as 10 years after graduation. Until then they were expected to do as they were told, work hard, stay in their place and earn their boss' favour.

As a result, Gen X are extremely resilient, self-reliant, independent, individualistic, and goal-oriented and do not typically seek the limelight. At work, they embrace risk, welcome challenges and are great at solving problems. They question authority, and while they do not trust businesses, they are loyal to people. When it comes to professional training, they prefer mentors outside of their organization rather than being taught from within.

Millennials and the Workplace Revolution

Millennials are the generation born between 1981 and 1995. They started off by dreaming of well-paying banking and consultancy jobs. Many of them studied Business, and those who studied Information Technology (IT) and Science, Technology, Engineering, and Mathematics (STEM) were considered "outsiders" with little prospects of making it big. And then the 2008 financial crisis happened. The older Millennials started graduating into unemployment and in response many of them decided to pursue further education, while the younger ones recalibrated their career plans and expectations. Software Engineering was the first industry to bounce back from the 2008 crisis, and money moved from public to private markets giving rise to the Venture Capital Boom. Governments ploughed money into entrepreneurship and innovation, and many Millennials leveraged those grants and projects as a safety net. As a result, Millennials are highly educated (many pursued more than one graduate degree), heavily digital (this was the area of growth that provided them with safety), well connected (they had to depend on each other for identifying and pursuing opportunities), highly entrepreneurial, and distrustful of large corporations (they felt loyalty was not reciprocated). They became used to having multiple "gigs" as a way to achieve independence, and despite their confident demenour they constantly felt the need to prove themselves.

I have already discussed in Chapter 3 how they transformed the workplace, so instead of repeating myself, I will tell you a story.

In 2006, as the first batch of Millennials was entering the workforce, I was leading an Employer Branding project for a leading **Investment Bank** that had recently merged with a commercial bank. They were worried this would "dilute" the brand in the eyes of perspective talent and that it would no longer be prestigious or competitive enough, so they decided to run a series of focus groups across top universities in the U.S.A. to better understand the impact of the merger on the brand.

During my very first focus group in Boston, a second-year finance student from Massachusetts Institute of Technology, told me that the merger was irrelevant, that he had already made up his mind not to join an investment bank. I asked why, after all his was the exact profile of students who would typically flock to the likes of **Lehman Brothers**, **Morgan Stanley**, **UBS**, **Merril Lynch**, **J.P. Morgan** or **Goldman Sachs**. He told me that he had already received an offer from another bank (not the client) but that he had decided to turn it down after attending their on-campus presentation. *"First of all, there was a very uninspiring guy who did all the talking. It was one big sales pitch with no time for us to ask questions, network, get the real scoop. But even worse, you know what they handed out to students as a giveaway after the event? Stress balls!!! Can you imagine? Stress balls! What are they trying to say? Do bankers have absolutely no imagination, or are they trying to send the message that the job will be so stressful that we need to start squeezing stress balls two years in advance?!"*

I was speechless. Having a job lined up at one of the most prestigious banks in the world barely halfway through college would have been a dream for most. Turning it down because of a stress ball made no sense to me at the time, especially as I remembered how difficult it had been for me to land my first paying job. I asked why the giveaway was so important, and he told me that everything an employer does when communicating to potential candidates is an indication of their culture, and if they cannot pay close attention to the message they send when *"trying to sell you a job"* then they will surely not pay any attention to you once you walk through the door. His peers around the table started to nod in agreement.

Although this deviated from what I was there to explore, I sensed something unprecedented in the discussion, so I asked what would constitute an acceptable giveaway. Participants started talking about **Google**'s brainteasers, and how they revealed imagination and appreciation for students' intellectual abilities. I took note and asked if there was anything else banks were doing "wrong". Another student jumped at the opportunity and said *"Banks have a dress code for on-campus interviews! We are students, we walk to school with our books and our bags. They cannot expect us to spend all day attending classes in a suit, and we cannot go home and change. Surely, they realize how crazy it is to expect us to be carrying our suit around. Campus is our turf; they should meet us as we are, tennis shoes and all."* Everyone agreed.

As I wrapped up the day, I reassured myself that an odd discussion would not matter that much with nine focus groups to go. Boy was I wrong! On every other campus from University of Chicago to Stamford, the message was the same: *"We want companies that show they care about us and take us for who we really are."* Back at the office I worried about how I would relay these findings to the client. I knew they were important, but they dangerously digressed from the topic that I was asked to explore.

To my surprise, as soon as I shared the students' feedback, the very senior group in the room stopped dead in their tracks. Instead of laughing or questioning them, the Global Head of HR said: *"Have we ordered the giveaways already? If yes, cancel them immediately! If not, put them on hold!"* *"And let students know that we will no longer have a suit requirement for on-campus interviews this coming season."* I remember everything being so fast, I could hardly believe my eyes. For another two hours the discussion focused on all the changes the bank would make to be more appealing to Millennial students. From one season to the next, the bank completely changed its on-campus recruitment practices. Competitors followed suit, and just like that, Millennials won the first of many battles.

I say first because the transformation was not limited to dress codes or giveaways. Once the economy started recovering, Millennial job seekers realized they had the power to choose where they wished to work, and it became the employer's job to entice them. Companies started asking students what they expected in terms of office environment, training, and responsibilities. "Day in the Life" videos, showing young talent pampered and welcomed into their new jobs started popping up all over the web. According to MTV's No Collars Study, upon entering the workforce 76 percent of Millennials said their boss could learn a lot from them, 66 percent said they should invent their own position at work, 90 percent said they wanted leadership to listen to their ideas and opinions, 33 percent said they preferred recognition over higher pay, and 50 percent said they would rather have no job than a job they hate. Other sources showed 80 percent said the work environment was more important than the size of their paycheck, 81 percent said they should set their own work schedules, and 90 percent said they deserved their dream job.

For Millennials, authenticity was paramount. "My expectation upon entering the workforce was that I would not have to dress up who I was but be my authentic self. This means everything from attire to not remaining silent in meetings. This was not always received as intended, especially with more traditional audiences, but substance of conversation and capabilities would usually overshadow face-value concerns," Agrim Singh, a Millennial from India who works for an international bank said.

Unlike Baby Boomers and Gen X who had to suffer in silence and accept whatever work environment they found themselves in, Millennials managed to transform theirs in their own image. Companies started offering fully stocked pantries with free food, gym membership, chill areas — even massage rooms — club houses and bars. The cubicle started disappearing, replaced by open floorplans. "I am not fussy about the office set-up beyond a disdain for cubicles. I work from a beanbag and am largely comfortable with an open setup that allows for more fluid interaction and opportunities for collaboration. The ideal office environment allows one to zone out and focus if they need to but have the avenue for groupthink and collaboration whenever the need arises," Agrim said.

As the first generation to grow up fully connected, Millennials saw the Internet as a tool for their larger desires. They simply assumed work–life balance, as flexible working conditions and the ability to integrate personal interests in their work schedule became the norm. *"Flexibility when it comes to work hours and physical office presence versus working from home are the ideal setup and a better use of my time. I don't focus well through the entire eight-hour stretch from 10 a.m. to 6 p.m., but work well in short sprints. This means I'm able to be more clinical and focused when I do sit in front of the computer to get work done, especially creative work, even if this means working outside traditional office hours,"* Agrim said.

Unlike Gen X, who felt they always had to watch their back, Millennials entered the workforce as the ultimate team players. Their value for collective action and *"Nobody Left Behind"* attitude was reflected in their need to be treated as collaborators in a process, and to work with their peers to create shared-value. They celebrated diversity and sought inclusive and progressive work environments, where everyone could be themselves without fear or discrimination.

While many articles over the years have described Millennials as job hoppers whom companies cannot rely on, I have always found them extremely committed and loyal when dedicated to an idea, a cause or a product they believe in. That said, without constant recognition, development, or challenging assignments they would leave.

"I am still with my first organization, having just started my eighth year and my fourth role. I expect an evolution of role every two to three years. I will leave when I can no longer actively contribute to the organization's achievement of strategic goals and am no longer learning rapidly," Joshua Gan, a Millennial from Singapore, told me.

The average expected tenure for Millennials was two to three years. *"There is no defined fixed time I expect to stay with an employer, but a key factor would definitely involve whether a role is going 'stale' and starts lacking fresh experiences. Expected wait before being promoted should not be longer than one to two years because I like seeing a year's achievements reflected in a tangible form, and it gives me confidence when the employer is on the same page,"* Agrim said.

Millennials did not want to fear for their job. Less likely to take big career risks or turn their personal lives inside out to make more money, they valued stability, security, supportive leaders and a friendly work environment well above pay and prestige. Millennials believed they could make a difference through their work, hence would not engage in work they deemed menial. Having a purpose became important in their day-to-day job. As Mark Zuckerberg **Facebook** Co-Founder and CEO said, *"Unless I feel like I am working on the most important problem that I can help with, then I am not going to feel good about how I am spending my time."* They wanted to earn money for doing what they are passionate about, and work for companies that shared their same values and took an ethical stand on issues of corporate social responsibility. Yet, as we have seen in Chapter 7, 60 percent of Millennials do not feel connected to their company's mission.

Unlike Gen X, Millennials were big planners and disliked uncertainty. They wanted an informal workplace but without the lack of structure. They wanted to create their own career path knowing that their employer had formal avenues in place to get them to where they wanted to be.

They expected a friendly, nurturing relationship with their boss, based on mutual trust, respect, recognition and collaboration. *"I appreciate anything that is not too heavy-handed or top-down by way of management and leadership. As an employee, of course I want to feel valued and heard, but in particular I love management and leadership styles that are collaborative and inclusive, giving everyone room to shine without micromanagement,"* Agrim said.

While for Baby Boomers and Gen X work was transactional, "you work, I pay you", Millennials sought continuous recognition and feedback in order to feel validated. *"Millennials grew up in a gamified reality (in virtual and real life). Instant and constant feedback is a fundamental need for them to ensure that they are on the right path. That their audience/clients/bosses are engaged. And that the fruit of their labor will not go to waste. While* some treat this as insecurity, Millennials see it as an implementation of the 'lean' test-and-learn mindset. Asking for feedback is a great way to learn and adapt as opposed to executing on a masterplan that loses relevance. In a volatile, uncertain, complex and ambiguous (VUCA) world, it's the only way to be," my husband Victor, who is a Millennial, told me once when I complained about the amount of feedback my Millennial team required.

Preparing someone for leadership meant autonomy, empowerment and the right amount of structure. They wanted full ownership of the mandate, yet, at the same time, they expected their boss to be there to help them and protect them if things went wrong. "Preparing someone for leadership means constantly stretching and challenging them beyond their standard job scope. This could entail additional projects to be exposed to different aspects of the organization, being sent for trainings, and having access to senior leadership as mentors. A pre-requisite for this should be full ownership of and exceeding expectations in one's current role and being curious and driven," Joshua said.

Finally, the way they felt about their work became much more important than their title. "To me it is simple: my aim is not to become the company CEO or Head of Innovation. It is all about how I feel, how much I am learning, and what options my current career trajectory keeps open for me. The moment I start feeling trapped or unhappy, it means the 'romance' is over," Victor told me multiple times while we were discussing his career aspirations.

Gen Z and the Post-Covid-19 Workplace

Gen Z are those born between 1996 and 2010 and they are the true digital natives. With abundant access to the Internet, smartphones and social media, they are exposed to a vast amount of information. At the same time, they grew up in a world facing unprecedented challenges that shaped their attitude towards life and career. I like to call Gen Z "**Pragmatic Idealists**", as they are both practical and have moral principles.

Gen Z openly recognizes that the main purpose of having a job is to earn money, get promoted and sustain a good life. But while compensation, leadership opportunities and career progression are important, they also understand that ignoring environmental and social causes is not a viable option. *"It is naïve to assume that any individual or conglomerate can avoid at least some form of social responsibility. I believe commitment to social causes to be an absolute necessity in order to sustain society and right the wrongs that past generations have enabled. In this day and age, it is almost impossible to be apolitical unless you come from a background of extreme privilege. The personal is, after all, political,"* Isabella Williams, a Gen Z from Australia, said to me. As a result, they are loyal to causes and principles and will only work with organizations aligned with their values. This is the generation that will not shy away from asking *"Why should I join your company? Where are your principles?"*

In 2018, I was moderating a panel of students between 15 and 18 years of age. They had been invited by an **Asian Bank** to talk about their career aspirations and expectations. The audience was Senior and Executive Management from Business, HR, Learning & Development, Marcom and Talent Acquisition, but the students did not seem the least intimidated. No suits — not even business casual — they came as themselves, with their jeans, t-shirts, tennis shoes, and their personality. As I stood there listening to their desire to make an impact, to change the world, to fix what has been "broken" by previous generations, I felt like going back in time and having a serious one-to-one with the 16-year-old me. At their age, all I worried about was seeing my friends, whether the boy I had a crush on felt the same about me, and to study enough to make good grades. Not these kids. At one point, a senior leader from the audience, asked them what it would take for them to consider a career in banking. I will always remember how one girl, 15 or 16 years of age, turned the question around. *"While I am studying, I am also mentoring startups that aim to solve some of the biggest challenges our society is facing today. If I stop doing that to join your organization instead, will I be able to make the same amount of impact or more, in the same amount of time?"* Naturally, everyone in the room remained quiet. That is the exact moment I decided I had to write this book.

"Commitment is what keeps my generation on track, the deeper our commitment to social causes the higher the chances that we will be extremely picky when it comes to our future employer because we will want to evaluate every little detail. If we find anything against our ideology, we won't be applying," Michael, a Gen Z from Indonesia, told me.

At work, Gen Z wants an innovative, creative and dynamic environment, with space for focused individual work as well as for open collaboration. The office is a place where they expect to socialize, build meaningful relationships, develop both as professionals and as human beings, and where they believe they can collectively drive change. As such, it also needs to guarantee their physical, mental and emotional well-being; plenty of encouragement and support, a pantry filled with healthy snacks and drinks. Recreational spaces where they can get up and walk around freely are a must. One interesting thing I heard from many Gen Z is their desire for natural light. Almost everyone I spoke to, told me they want an office with lots of windows, and little artificial lighting.

When it comes to working hours, Covid-19 has cemented Gen Z's expectation to be able to work anywhere anytime. They want careers that are outcome-oriented as opposed to time-driven. This will cause a significant change in how people plan their lives. I believe, in time, we will see many Gen Z moving away from big urban areas and repopulate smaller towns. After all, if you do not have to physically be in an office, there is no need to trade nature or proximity to family for a good job!

Unlike Millennials, who expected a peer-like relationship with their superiors, Gen Z seems to be okay with keeping healthy boundaries but believes that a friendly relationship benefits culture and performance. *"I would like to go out for lunch with my boss not 'for the sakes of it' but because of his genuine interest to get to know me better as a person and know what is happening in my personal life. I would work better under my manager's guidance if we had a relationship where we share each other's holistic view on life, where both of us are more vulnerable, and where we are aware of each other's personalities, likes and dislikes,"* Daniel Foo Jun Wei, a Gen Z from Singapore, told me.

Forty-eight percent of Gen Z said being the youngest in the workplace makes them nervous, and 72 percent are intimidated by the older generations, predominantly because of the respect they expect, their display of power, their stern and distant attitude, and their lack of patience. 54 percent would prefer a Millennial manager, who they feel would better understand them and their needs. *"It is important to have an empathic boss who is genuinely interested in you and is not too serious and strict. I would like to be able to feel that I am heard and that criticism can go both ways without affecting the relationship,"* Daniel said.

According to the *XYZ@Work 2020 Multigenerational Workforce Study*, 72 percent of Gen Z who are still in school believe that they will find it challenging to work or be managed by colleagues from different age groups, predominantly because of **different mindsets**, **hierarchy**, and **communication**. *"They may not understand that the world has changed from the time they started working and may not accept the new paradigms, newer methods and approach to things. We, younger people want to try new approaches to solve the world's problems, while the older generations keep resisting change,"* a Gen Z from the U.S.A. said. Gen Z also fear that they will be pressured to use old guidelines and processes, to work on tedious tasks, and that they will be stuck in a dead-end job.

When it comes to tenure, Gen Z are open to staying for as long as there is alignment in values, they are happy, love what they do, and feel they are making a significant contribution. *"I hope to stay with my first employer for a minimum of one to two years. If a position truly fulfilled me and I believed it would allow for potential upward mobility both within the same company or outside of it, I would stay for as long as I believe it to be beneficial to my quality of life and professional satisfaction. I would likely leave a position if a workplace environment was too individualistic and pessimistic, as I value collaboration and goal-oriented performance,"* Isabella said. Gen Z would also leave a company with too much politics, repetitive work and lack of challenging projects, workplace conflicts, favoritism, inability to contribute, and lack of work–life balance or flexibility.

Gen Z think that what they lack in practical experience they can make up for with enthusiasm, open-mindedness and work ethics, and they seek employers who believe in their potential, will mentor them and are willing to facilitate their on-the-job learning. *"I have always recognized the value of a strong mentor-mentee relationship, and many of the professionals I currently look up to have spoken of the myriad benefits of such an experience. They have cited their mentor's trust, confidence and compassion for the learning process as pivotal to their professional development. The ability to both understand and facilitate on-the-job training for those in entry-level positions can lead only to growth, innovation and a heightened sense of community within the workplace,"* Isabella said.

When it comes to development, Gen Z prefer a lighter load and more training at the beginning. This allows them to assimilate into the culture and get to know the team. Subsequently, they want to be able to work on challenging tasks and passion-infused projects without micromanagement, but still able to candidly reach out to their manager or team members if they need support.

Leadership to Gen Z means the opportunity to utilize and experiment with different styles of management, forms of delegation, and problem-solving with a sustained emphasis on the bigger picture. *"Preparation for leadership means the cultivation of skills which enable strong attention to detail without losing sight of the grand scheme of things. Above all else, preparation for leadership means allowing someone the space and compassion for practice, for trial and error, for failure, because from failure comes growth through lived experience,"* Isabella said.

Finally, Gen Z believe that you learn by sharing and discussing, so they like the opportunity to meet, either virtually or in person, as frequently as possible (even daily) with colleagues, managers and leaders. The goal is to share opinions, constructive feedback and ideas about ongoing projects. During these meetings everyone should be transparent and be given equal voice without any hard feelings.

Chapter 15

The Opposing Definition of Respect

One thing Baby Boomers frequently complain about is how young employees show no respect towards their generation. This issue with "respect" is clearly a major source of conflict, especially in Asia, where society dictates elders be honored and held in high esteem. However, all of the Millennials and Gen Z whom I spoke with, profoundly disagree, insisting that their interactions with their managers are not contemptuous — to the contrary. So, the question is not whether there is a lack of respect, but whether the different generations define respect in the same way.

In 2009, I was in London sharing global talent trends with a group of senior HR professionals from large multinational companies, and it was not long before the issue surrounding Millennials, their defiance towards authority and their lack of boundaries was brought up as a major challenge for most employers around the table. I specifically remember the anecdote shared by the Global Head of Employer Branding of one of the **Investment Banks**. One of their interns, a bright young man from an Ivy League School with great vision and vast ambitions, had decided, shortly after joining, to share his big idea directly with the Global CEO. He had asked his line manager to make an introduction but was told it would not be possible, so he started emailing the CEO's assistant asking her to set up a meeting. After receiving no response to his many emails, he decided to take the lift to the top floor, walk straight into the CEO's office, sit down and — "short of patting him on the shoulder" — start sharing his idea. In today's environment, this may not seem so terribly far-fetched, but this is recent; back then this type of behavior was not only uncommon but highly discouraged. The company representative went on to share how this incident took everyone by surprise, particularly in an environment where people — even Senior Management — would make themselves really small if they accidentally ran into the CEO in the elevator. Not yet ready to embrace this generational shift, they had to take action against the intern. Walking up to the CEO as if he were a peer — in that bank, at that time — defied social norms, was seen as "insubordination" and considered "highly disrespectful". On the other hand, the young man struggled to understand how being innovative, showing initiative and not taking "no" for an answer could reap anything but a reward.

The issue here lies in the opposing definition of respect particularly, once again, between Baby Boomers and Millennials. For Baby Boomers, respect for authority is shown through **deference** — or polite submission — and more weight given to their opinions. Gen X do not expect deference (they instead define respect as being held in esteem and listened to) but were taught how to behave "appropriately" around their elders, hence respect is typically not an issue between Gen X and Baby Boomers. Millennials, on the other hand, reject deference flat out, seeing it as an unnecessary formality and a waste of time; and Gen Z merely understand it but are open to being accommodating: *"Seniors or bosses expect respect from their subordinates. I guess they feel our gestures and attitudes show them how much we value the title they bear. We don't want to give our supervisor the wrong impression so we will need to show respect their way,"* a Gen Z told me.

The different attitude towards deference, can easily be linked back to family dynamics. Let's stop and think for a minute about father-son interaction in the 1950s and 1960s. Baby Boomers' relationship with a father was founded on tough-love. They could speak only when spoken to, and were castigated if they misbehaved. Punishment was an act of love; it was for their own good — it would make them strong. The father was somebody they admired, someone whose shoes they felt they would never quite fill, and this translated into **reverential fear**. So, it is only normal that when young Baby Boomers joined an organization working with people who reminded them of their own father, they would respond to these senior colleagues in a similar way. Deference was the way to show respect, back then.

Millennials, however, were not raised to treat their fathers with deference or a healthy dose of fear. Their relationship with their parents often blurs into friendship — they involve them in their private lives, enjoy spending time together and talk to them as equals. They are encouraged to have conversations about everything and anything, and to express their point of view honestly and openly.

When Millennials joined the workforce, they approached older colleagues directly and spontaneously. In fact, Millennials are the first generation who is comfortable working alongside older generations. And why shouldn't they be? Unlike Gen X and Baby Boomers, they were not raised to fear authority but to be themselves around their elders. Millennials believe that respect must be earned and that it goes both ways — as much in the workplace as it does at home. It is no surprise then, that Millennials also often complain about a lack of respect from the older generations. And while Baby Boomers hold the young generations' failure to show deference in contempt, to Millennials being honest and direct *is* a sign of respect. *"'I respect you enough to tell you the truth, to involve you in my thinking process, to call it how I see it.' After all, this saves everybody time, and instead of beating around the bush and being artificially polite or evasive, we can focus directly on the issues we need to resolve and get more work done. To do this, trust is required, and trust comes with respect,"* Victor, a Millennial, told me.

The solution is to openly acknowledge the different interpretations and expressions of **Respect** by providing work teams with an understanding of generational context. What does each generation expect when it comes to "respect", and should we label any behavior that differs from our expectation as "disrespectful"?

I believe in respecting those who earn my respect. If people of authority do something to lose my respect, I will no longer hold them in high regard.

Gen Z from Singapore

Our mission to challenge the status quo is often mislabeled as "lack of respect"

Millennial from The Netherlands

Figure 19

Chapter 16

How Parenting Styles Affect Workplace Leadership

By talking to people across generations, you will discover that parenting styles follow ever-changing trends and most parents will adapt their own individual approach to the dominant trend at the time. However, not many consider that the way we are raised affects our response to authority, and influences our leadership style. So how has the childhood of Baby Boomers, Gen X, Millennials and Gen Z shaped them as leaders?

Baby Boomers and Authoritarian Parents

Before we talk about the leadership style of the Baby Boomers, I want to take a step back and look at that of the **Traditionalists**, the generation that came before them. This is what most Baby Boomers experienced upon entering the workforce.

During the years following World War II, the best leadership training was thought to come from the Army. In many countries, ex-military employees were in high demand for leadership tracks due to their ability to set up structures and manage large organizations. Since many of the tasks and systems to be managed were relatively straightforward and complexity came from scale, this was probably the right thing to do for a while. As the knowledge economy matured, and organizations started operating in more complex ecosystems and information architectures, different type of skillset — such as strong EQ or a deep specialization in STEM — were required. This created an engineer-business divide within organizations that digital transformation is still coping with today. To address this, flatter and more matrixed organizations emerged, and the Control and Command style of leadership became no longer relevant nor effective. While young Baby Boomers were subjected to it under the Traditionalists — and naturally most emulated it to some extent as they progressed in their own careers — it does not mean they enjoyed it or subscribed to it.

Baby Boomers were generally raised in a traditional authoritarian household, with a man established as the head of the family. Here the leader-father made all the major decisions without much consultation with the rest of the family. This structure was replicated in the workplace as a hierarchical pyramid of bosses and subordinates. Orders were passed down from the top to the bottom levels — you could be both a subordinate to those "above" you in the pyramid, and a boss to those "below" you.

Baby Boomers had to fight to work, succeed and prosper. Because of their vast experience and the many challenges and crisis situations they have faced in their lifetime, their general attitude towards leadership is "they've seen and done it all". As a result, they tend to be more prescriptive in how they counsel or direct others. As managers, they tend to have a paternalistic approach and want to see their team members as family. This means they often nurture or punish the way a parent would.

As leaders, Baby Boomers are team players, resilient, fiercely loyal, and have strong respect for the chain of command. They believe there is a price to pay for success, and it often involves putting work first and enjoying life later: this makes them the original "workaholics". They feel the need to "set the example", so what they expect from others is no different than what they expect first and foremost from themselves. *"My first boss, a Boomer, was the most dedicated and committed person I ever met. At some point he got cancer, but that seriously tough man showed up EVERY SINGLE DAY, even while on chemo!!! Toughest guy in the world. He led by example. He didn't quit on himself, on us, on the job. He was 'The Man'! "* Bill, a Gen X, said.

Baby Boomers often believe that authority is legitimized by their position and role in the organization, and that their knowledge and experience are of great benefit to others. They have a view on virtually any topic, as well as precise beliefs about what is right or wrong based on their experience interacting with the world. This can make them come across as rigid, stuck in their ways and reluctant to change.

"Today we see two types of Baby Boomers: the first are those who have effectively retired from everything, hence their views are immovable, prescriptive and intense. They will have an opinion on almost every subject and will sound like experts. They are great storytellers and they are financially set for life. The second are those who are interested to redefine themselves and are open to change because they still need to survive and compete effectively with the young for jobs. Both types are useful as they bring different benefits to the table. We need our sages and our mentors. Their experience through time teaches us lessons we would otherwise not have known. On the extreme end, there are vast numbers of Boomers who should be re-employed, re-trained and re-mobilized as they are healthier, more willing to learn and connect. They offer critical talent gaps which we still face with or without Covid-19," Stephen, a Baby Boomer, said.

In 2016, I was running a workshop for a leading **Financial Services Group** looking to unveil its Employer Value Proposition. The CEO was in the room, alongside two dozen senior managers from Marketing, HR, Employer Branding, Learning & Development and Communications. The group started a discussion around the need to articulate the company's Purpose to resonate with young talent. At one point the CEO, a Baby Boomer, stood up impatiently and said: *"I don't get it. Why two hours to discuss our purpose?!? We are a bank. Our purpose is simple. Make money!"* And although he was not entirely wrong, through this one response, this leader displayed the four traits that the young generations resent the most: lack of empathy, old-style mentality, being out of touch with current times, and resistance to change.

"What Boomers lack most is the ability to listen actively. They prefer to hear what they want to hear. This typically results in communication gaps and intensifies the generational divide when they interact with Millennials. They are excellent storytellers and are able to contextualize many situations, but

they need to be able to also appreciate and empathize with the circumstances that the younger generation might be facing, instead of dismissing them as 'entitlement' issues or circumstances which only plague the young and naïve," Stephen continued.

It is important to note that while most Baby Boomers have a traditional leadership style with a "top down" approach, this has been tempered significantly over the last decade or two and many Baby Boomers today are very effective in using a "bottoms up" leadership style. Some of the most inspiring leaders I have ever met were Baby Boomers, Paul Polman, former CEO of Unilever, being one of them.

"There are many examples of Boomers who were not bound by tradition. They created innovative new technologies and new companies. An example is Bill Gates. There are many others. Some younger people look at Boomers as selfish in accumulating as much wealth as they can. That may be true, but I think they either forget or don't know about all the charitable work and massive donations of their wealth many Boomers are making. And these Boomers are making great progress solving some of the world's worst problems — disease, clean drinking water, poverty," Kent, a Baby Boomer, explained.

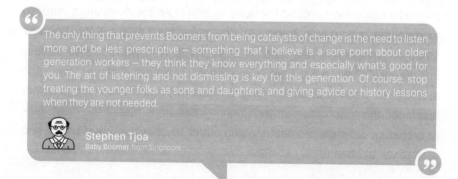

The only thing that prevents Boomers from being catalysts of change is the need to listen more and be less prescriptive — something that I believe is a sore point about older generation workers — they think they know everything and especially what's good for you. The art of listening and not dismissing is key for this generation. Of course, stop treating the younger folks as sons and daughters, and giving advice or history lessons when they are not needed.

Stephen Tjoa
Baby Boomer from Singapore

Figure 20

Gen X and Uninvolved Parents

As the smaller bridging generation between the Baby Boomers and Millennials, Gen X was responsible for triggering a healthy shift in leadership styles. Unlike their predecessors and successors, they were born in what is often referred to as the *"Anti-child Era"* when rising divorce rates and more women going to work meant young Gen X had to spend a lot of time on their own and unsupervised, earning them the name *"Latchkey Kids"*. *"Most of us survived on our own, we learned how to cook, clean, do laundry, interact, socialize, win AND lose, and respect others. I am also fairly certain most Gen X were put into a situation at some point during their formative years where they had to be fiercely independent in order to survive,"* Bill, Gen X from the U.S.A. shared with me.

Gen X's childhood was famously lax, with kids free of the discipline that restricted previous generations, and allowed to roam the countryside without the safety restrictions of the next (such as the personal protective gear that became widely used by Millennial children). As a result, they grew up self-reliant and comfortable with change. They knew what they were responsible for and what was required of them, and they were expected to do it without reminders or directions. As a Gen X teenager, for example, I never had to "cut school". If I did not feel like going for whatever reason, I could just decide to stay home. My parents would not question it because they trusted my judgment. They made it abundantly clear that my "job" was to study, learn and get good grades, and if I failed to do so I — and I alone — would pay the consequences of my poor choices. But they never micromanaged the process. I had the freedom to achieve my goals *my way*. To them, this was part of growing up.

When Gen X entered the workforce in the 1980s and 1990s, they inherited the success-driven ethic of working hard and striving for good pay. Through this combination of a rough-and-tumble childhood and the drive to succeed, they forged a more collaborative work environment, where the distinction between senior and junior roles was still clear, but the communication between the two flowed more easily. As leaders, Gen X are entrepreneurial and extremely independent. They are hands-off, setting the goal but allowing their employees to achieve what is expected of them in their own way. "*Better ask for forgiveness than ask for permission,*" I was told by many of my Gen X managers throughout the years.

This leadership style, however, is not the most effective when managing the young generations who expect guidance, step-by-step direction and constant feedback. I experienced this on my own skin. As a Gen X, I managed people the way I wanted to be managed: letting them know that I had their back but giving them ample space to reach the outcome; and staying out of their hair throughout the process, but making myself fully available to support when needed and to step in to solve problems. I later realized it required a particular type of Millennial to thrive under these conditions, and halfway through my career I had to learn how to become the very manager I would not have wanted for myself.

As a result, Gen X is often battling between leadership styles. "*Gen X leaders are very conscious. They spend a lot of time thinking about how they lead. They distinguish leadership from management too — management is about individuals in the chain and more direct relationships, whereas leadership is a bit more aligned to role modelling and their public selves,*" Tamara Singh, a Gen X from Singapore, said.

Because of the competition Gen X faced upon entering the workforce, they are known to be wary of everyone and generally non-trusting. "*They are the in-the trenches type of leaders, not loudmouth bosses who subscribe to 'do as I say not as I do'. No job is beneath them, they are the 'been there done that' and while in theory it should garner them respect, it doesn't always,*" Bill explained. Unlike Baby Boomers, Gen X leaders do not feel the need to impart their knowledge or wisdom but, strongly ingenious, they have a way around almost every problem and put their skills to the service of the organization. "*Gen X are living between the transition era of old school and high technological advancement. They understand both, are good at decision-making, know how to solve problems, and when technology can't help they can use old school methods,*" a Gen Z from Malaysia said.

"*Most of the Gen X leaders I see around me are usually hard workers and have made it to the higher levels of the organization. They are mature enough not to feel threatened, are willing to share their experiences and guide their teams. They are still craving for their boss' approval and recognition and are usually 'good little soldiers' in how they perform. Some may feel threatened by the newer generation but most don't, simply because after many years they've come to understand that there are other priorities in life, and that rank and title don't always equate to happiness and satisfaction,*" Sarina, a Gen X from South Africa told me.

Many consider Gen X the most under-recognized generation in the workforce, but according to the *2018 Global Leadership Forecast Study* it plays a critical role in leadership as organizations grapple with digital transformation. Gen X was trained by Baby Boomers and is tech savvy. This makes Gen X the generation that Gen Z, Millennials and Baby Boomers have the least challenge collaborating with (besides their own). As "cuspers", they are viewed as the bridge between Traditional and New Age mindsets.

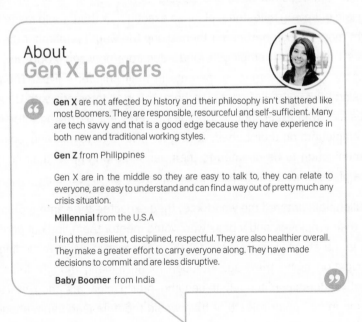

About
Gen X Leaders

66 **Gen X** are not affected by history and their philosophy isn't shattered like most Boomers. They are responsible, resourceful and self-sufficient. Many are tech savvy and that is a good edge because they have experience in both new and traditional working styles.

Gen Z from Philippines

Gen X are in the middle so they are easy to talk to, they can relate to everyone, are easy to understand and can find a way out of pretty much any crisis situation.

Millennial from the U.S.A

I find them resilient, disciplined, respectful. They are also healthier overall. They make a greater effort to carry everyone along. They have made decisions to commit and are less disruptive.

Baby Boomer from India 99

Figure 21

Millennials and "Helicopter Parents"

Millennials are the product of a shift from an adult-centric to a child-centric society. Their Baby Boomer parents pushed the boundaries, tried alternative parenting styles and had a much more lenient approach to disciplining children than Traditionalists or the Greatest Generation. Also referred to as "Helicopter Parents" because of their constant hovering, Baby Boomers were supportive, friendly, omni-present and had big ambitions for their children. They believed that building a child's self-esteem is the key to their future success and took positive reinforcement to the next level by giving out participation trophies. This earned Millennials the name "Trophy Kids" and, according to many, lead to a generation of narcissistic and perennially disappointed adults. At the same time, this also made Millennials the first teens who did not have a need to rebel against their parents.

Millennial parents got involved in every little detail of their lives, enrolled them in numerous activities and closely monitored their every movement. They laid out every milestone, planned exactly how they would reach it, and fought most of their battles for them along the way. I remember the many stories I heard from employers and educators between 2006 and 2012 about the overinvolvement of parents in their children's lives. They were choosing their course of study for them, trying to intercede with University professors when they got bad grades, even went as far as interviewing with employers on their behalf, asking for offer letters and any job-related communication to be directed to them, and showing up at their children's future place of work requesting to be taken on an office tour.

As Millennials entered the workforce, they expected the same type of care from their employer, and a boss who would mentor them, lay out goals and provide the structure necessary for them to reach it, while rewarding their participation along the way. Although many initially thought Millennials lacked leadership potential, it became pretty clear as they started to assume more senior roles that they would redefine leadership altogether. Their need to have their voices heard led to the demise of the pyramid hierarchy, replaced by a flat management structure meant to facilitate decision-making and communication.

Figure 22

Millennials are the first generation of influencer leaders. Their approach is not to be appointed but to lead through creating **followership** — online and offline. Furthermore, their organizations are way more complex and self-governing. Meritocracy and influence have a much bigger role to play than in the past where leadership was more of a "role". Millennial leaders are authentic. They are the ones you can relate to, not "unreachable" ones whose shoes you think you will never be able to fill.

"We are largely risk-averse and highly authentic — we won't differentiate between our professional and personal selves and value expression and independent thought. There's a great emphasis on self-care and well-being, and consequently on work–life balance. There is a consistent effort on the learning and development front. But most importantly, Millennial Leaders get their team to bond around a shared purpose and know that the collective is a catalyst towards achieving any goal," Agrim, a Millennial, said.

Mark Zuckerberg, one of the first prominent Millennial leaders, defined Leadership in three words: **Empowerment**, **Sense of Purpose** and **Connection**.

Gen Z and "Stealth Fighter Parents"

Parents are the biggest influencers on Gen Z's educational and career choices. This may not seem noteworthy, after all, parents have steered and directed their kids' choices for centuries. In thinking so however, we forget that it is not only the children who change during generational shifts, parents and parenting styles do, too. Gen Z's parents, Gen X, are very different from the authoritarian parents of the Baby Boomers or the hovering parents of the Millennials. Neil Howe, described Gen X as *"Stealth Fighter Parents"*, surveilling from a distance and only getting involved in case of serious issues. Unlike *"Helicopter Parents"*, who tried to protect their Millennial children from hardship at any cost, Gen X have raised their kids to be more autonomous and independent. At the same time, Gen X-parents are more invested in supporting their children when needed, to discover who they are and what they would enjoy, as opposed to taking the decision for them. As a result, Gen Z do not blindly follow what moms and dads demand of them, they willingly and proactively go to them for advice.

Naturally, since Gen Z are still young and far from taking on leadership positions within organizations, it is impossible to know with certainty what type of leaders they will be. However, with the vast amount of information they have been exposed to and the healthy dose of skepticism instilled upon them by their Gen X parents, what is pretty certain is that Gen Z will be questioning and redefining the concept of Leadership even further. I have spoken to and interviewed hundreds of Gen Z about what leaders they think they will be. Many said they feel skeptical towards the term "Leader" which has being thrown around and bestowed upon undeserving people — particularly in schools — who then developed a "sense of superiority and authority over others, a false sense of competency and accountability, pride, denial, and arrogance." All this while many young people who possess true leadership qualities — because of lack of support in their homes or schools — never developed the self-confidence to become one. *"True leadership is not a position, but the ability to take up a challenge because you want to serve and help others, regardless of fame, recognition, money or any other form of personal gain,"* Daniel, a Gen Z, said to me.

Others told me that because Gen Z's future is likely to be affected by pressing social and environmental issues, they will lead with more **empathy**, **awareness** and **love for the world**, At the same time, we can expect media fragmentation to be reflected in a vast array of different approaches to leadership. "*Worst-case scenario: a chaotic lack of consistency. Best-case scenario: diverse approaches will lead to some discomfort and trial-and-error, but then give way to innovative styles of leadership which are in a constant state of revision as a means of improving quality of work,*" Isabella, a Gen Z, said.

"*To be honest, I can't say what kind of leaders my generation will be, because we are not there yet. But every day I am amazed by how people can be terrifyingly smart and surprisingly dumb. Since society is nowadays more fluid and dynamic, I would say my generation will lead the world with **goal-based leadership**. This means, in facing the next challenges, we will do whatever it takes to eliminate the problem using any possible avenue so that mankind can survive. The main focus for us will be to reach that goal,*" Michael, a Gen Z said when I asked him what kind of leadership the world can expect from Gen Z.

WHAT GEN Z WANT
IN A LEADER

- ✓ Open-minded
- ✓ Shares the credit
- ✓ Recognizes success
- ✓ Leads by example
- ✓ Empowering
- ✓ Inspiring
- ✓ Authentic
- ✓ Relatable
- ✓ Committed to vision and purpose

Figure 23

Fears and Concerns of the Multigenerational Workforce

When we look at Baby Boomers with their experience, Gen X with their resourcefulness, Millennials with their confidence, and Gen Z with their conviction, it is hard to imagine any of them having feelings of self-doubt. Yet, every generation has its insecurities when it comes to their role in today's workplace. Baby Boomers fear **becoming obsolete**, Gen X **plateauing in their career**, Millennials **being sandwiched between generations**, and Gen Z **not being taken seriously**. Furthermore, both

WHY OLDER GEN ARE INTIMIDATING

 They are eloquent and experienced. They seem to know everything about life and when you talk to them it feels like you are listening to a live history book.

Gen Z from Philippines

They are well regarded and have a lot of power which they hold over your head. They are also well-connected and know how to play office politics, so you have to be careful.

Millennial from Singapore

Engaging them requires a certain protocol, and you need to be careful with your choice of words. It's hard to connect with them because they are rarely authentic.

Gen X from Italy

Figure 24

younger and older generations are worried about the assumptions that others make because of their age, and the need to figure out how best to interact with other generations.

Sixty percent of Gen Z, 26 percent of Millennials and 17 percent of Gen X feel intimidated by older colleagues because of their **experience**, **knowledge**, **rank**, and **power**.

At the same time, 12 percent of Baby Boomers, 9 percent of Gen X and 12 percent of Millennials feel intimidated by younger employees because of their **energy**, **know-it-all attitude**, **ability to learn quickly**, and **tech-savviness**.

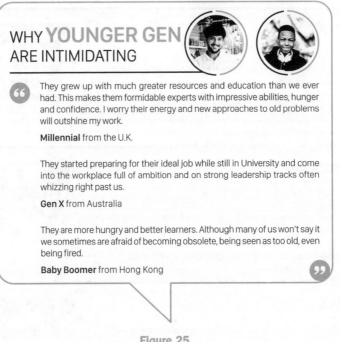

WHY **YOUNGER GEN**
ARE INTIMIDATING

"
They grew up with much greater resources and education than we ever had. This makes them formidable experts with impressive abilities, hunger and confidence. I worry their energy and new approaches to old problems will outshine my work.
Millennial from the U.K.

They started preparing for their ideal job while still in University and come into the workplace full of ambition and on strong leadership tracks often whizzing right past us.
Gen X from Australia

They are more hungry and better learners. Although many of us won't say it we sometimes are afraid of becoming obsolete, being seen as too old, even being fired.
Baby Boomer from Hong Kong
"

Figure 25

During the many interviews, studies and conversations I have had over the years with professionals from all walks of life, what emerged clear as day is that **every generation is silently facing a secret battle**. In my 2020-study I asked more than 1000 professionals to describe the hurdles they experience on a day-to-day basis because of the age group they belong to. You can find their most common answers in Figure 26.

THE CHALLENGES EACH
GENERATION FACES IN THE WORKPLACE

Baby Boomer

- Overcoming old mental models
- Lack of tech knowledge
- Being physically slow
- Not learning as fast as the younger generations
- The belief our ideas are out of date
- Being treated as a fixed asset and being passed for promotions and recognition
- Having sufficient creativity and energy to engage and keep up with 3 younger generations

Gen X

- Staying relevant
- Approaching a new age bracket and the bias attached to it
- The belief that we are by now at the final stages of our career
- Hitting a ceiling in terms of advancement and earning potential
- Being on the cusp: too old for the new gen and still too young for executive management
- Lack of visibility: we are the lost generation and people don't care what we have to say
- Ageism when looking for jobs

Millennial

- Getting our point across to older leaders
- Being sandwiched between generations
- Being paid based on experience instead of on skills and talents
- Balancing work and family while building financial stability
- Dealing with institutional power
- Being thought of as disrespectful, spoiled and difficult
- Not being respected

Gen Z

- Being underestimated because of our lack of experience
- The perception we are spoon-fed individuals, stubborn and impatient
- The pressure and use the right approach with three older generations
- Having limited opportunities
- Sharing our vision for the future, yet nobody listens
- Knowing the future depends on us
- Being stuck doing menial work

Figure 26

FEARS IN A MULTIGENERATIONAL
WORKPLACE

 The fear I may be losing connection with the younger generations and may have to share the consequences of their over-reaching. That they don't have the bandwidth for my notes of caution.

Baby Boomer from India

 I fear ageism when finding jobs. Even if I remain very current in my skills and attitudes, a 28-year-old with a good set of skills would trump me in a head-to-head job competition simply due to age.

Gen X from Australia

I fear that being sandwiched between the different generations will make it hard for me to meet my own needs of transparency in communication, challenging the status quo, achievement and recognition.

Millennial from Singapore

 I fear being underestimated, compared to others, and not heard. For Gen Z it started in elementary school all the way through higher education, and we are sick of it.

Gen Z from Indonesia

Figure 27

Team leaders and talent professionals, who have to liaise and engage people across every age group, are aware of the challenges employees face in a multigenerational workplace, yet often fear not being up to the task in solving them. Effectively communicating with every generation, keeping everyone engaged and motivated, aligning the different working styles and preferences is not easy. The biggest fears that HR professionals face when trying to harmonize the Multigenerational Workforce are shown in Figure 28.

FEARS OF HR PROFESSIONALS IN A MULTIGENERATIONAL WORKPLACE

- Being misunderstood
- Alienating certain groups of people
- Being unable to bring all generations under one vision
- Inability to accommodate everyone's expectations
- Failing to ensure fairness
- Over sensitivity to open debate caused by political correctness
- Fear of offending people

Figure 28

And they are right. Things are tense and there are a lot of hidden — and often unexpected — sensitivities around this topic.

To illustrate this point, I want to share a personal experience. In May of 2020, as I was halfway through writing this book and confined at home because of the Covid-19 lockdown, a New York Times story titled "Demand Has Surged for Software That Can Monitor Employees Working From Home" popped up on my Facebook newsfeed. I do not usually interact with public posts, but this time because of how passionately I feel about micromanagement *not* being the way to ensure productivity, I decided to comment. I was concurrently playing with my three kids — aged one, two and five at the time — so I did not give too much thought to what I wrote or how I wrote it. Within seconds, I received a reply from a Baby Boomer accusing me of being generationally insensitive. Naturally, I took it personally, so I responded and clarified the intended meaning of my message. After a brief exchange we realized we were on the same side, I discovered she is an inspired and experienced professional, and we later connected about her potential contribution to this book.

I have decided to share this story, and the actual Facebook exchange in Figure 29 on the next page, to show how sensitive people can be to negative stereotypes. Sadly, until they are discussed and addressed, conflicts between generations are likely to persist even when people have the best intentions. If someone like me, who has spent most of her professional career helping to bring generations together by encouraging empathy, curiosity and understanding, caused this type of reaction with a casual Facebook message, imagine how many similar situations may arise in the workplace each day. I was lucky to have had an opportunity to explain myself because I was openly called out. But this is not likely to happen in the workplace, and without the opportunity to discuss and clarify, mutual resentment builds up making it difficult for people to collaborate fruitfully.

The great news is that despite all these fears and concerns, 100 percent of Baby Boomers and 98 percent of Gen X said they enjoy working with younger generations. Similarly, 92 percent of Gen X, 95 percent of Millennials and 90 percent of Gen Z said they enjoy working with older generations. This is a very important pre-requisite to achieve workplace harmony. Imagine how much precious energy could be preserved, and how many unnecessary conflicts could be avoided, if organizations showed some genuine commitment and took some actionable steps to putting these worries to rest.

Rachele Focardi Absolutely the last thing employers should do. With many organizations now redefining their work environments to attract talent and position themselves as ideal places to work, organizations with such backward practices will eventually find themselves struggling to attract and retain the talent they need. The Future of Work is here and Micromanagement and Control & Command style that characterized the older generations has no place in it.
Plus, everyone's context in this time of crises is different. Many people have kids to take care of and home-schooling on top of their job and are barely coping, while others - perhaps single or with grown up kids - may have a lot of time on their hands and find solace in their work. Everyone's situation is unique and there is no one answer, so the best thing an employer can do is show empathy by giving employees space and time to figure out their new normal and show interest in their wellbeing and mental health. We are all human beings and we are all in a situation none of us chose. Employers who treat employees with distrust and like property or robots may get away with it while people struggle to keep their jobs - or find new ones - but eventually will be pegged for what they are: inhumane and toxic environments that have no place in a Millennial and Gen Z dominated world (and I say this as a Gen X).

👍❤ 36

Like - Reply - 12w - Edited

Rachele Focardi agree with you on the tracking as if we were children. I've worked remotely and managed teams of remote people for >20 yrs....as well as advised other leaders in this time of SIP, that one can tell whether someone is getting their work done overall when they are remote. Most people working at home do more than expected of them for many reasons... self-driven desire to perform well, ensure others don't think they are not working...fewer interruptions. Of course, in this SIP scenario, there is an added level of background concern or anxiety as the remote working is on a massive scale with less in office support and a greater need for making connections because of that...and there are different factors such as home schooling etc., adding complexity. You should know that I am at the end of the Baby Boomer generation....your issues are with a type/style of management which no one desires, Baby Boomers or otherwise.... Millennial, Gen XYZ. A little grace on your part in acknowledging what those who've come before you have accomplished and what is now available to you and what they have to offer will also enable a non-toxic humane environment. Lumping classes of people together and assuming they think and are alike does not

Like - Reply - 12w

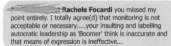

Rachele Focard I have made it my life's work to bridge the generational divide in the workplace and have been doing so for 15 years with governments and organizations all around the world. While there is a lot to be learned from all generations there is a specific direction the world is moving towards when it come to the future of work and spying on your employees and controlling them from a distance ain't it.

Like - Reply - 12w - Edited

Rachele Focardi you missed my point entirely. I totally agree(d) that monitoring is not acceptable or necessary.....your insulting and labelling autocratic leadership as 'Boomer' think is inaccurate and that means of expression is ineffective...

Like - Reply - 12w

Rachele Focardi Again ...as I've said twice.....spying is not ok. I often quote Mary Barra, CEO of GM who has said she doesn't see the need for a dress code...because if she can't trust colleagues to know how to trust, how can she trust them to make decisions.

Like - Reply - 12w

Rachele Focardi And hey ...she is a Baby Boomer and a CEO

Like - Reply - 12w

Rachele Focardi perhaps I expressed myself poorly. I absolutely agree that labelling and stereotypes do more harm than good, but it is a fact that Control and Command is a leadership style that characterized the Traditionalist and Baby Boomer Generation. This does not mean that all Baby Boomers adopted it or that they enjoyed the organizations that embraced it and propagated it. I am also not blaming or pegging the micromanagement this article is about to the Baby Boomers today. In fact, some of the most inspiring leaders I have ever met are Baby Boomers who have made it their mission to grow, train and enable young talent to bring about impact and innovation. I am writing a book on how to bring the generations together at work that will be published internationally later this year. And the entire points of it is exactly to encourage people across all generations to challenge labels and stereotypes.

Like - Reply - 12w - Edited

Rachele Focardi well that was much more gracefully stated....thank you. Baby Boomers brought much of the change...in my humble opinion Command and Control was also rebelled against generations before now including quite a few baby boomers.... that is also a fact which should be acknowledged.... my point is that if one is to challenge for the better, which I've done since exiting the womb thanks to my parents.....acclimates more by promoting what's good to better without bashing what came before.....that is the art...in the current political environment that civility is being abandoned...effectively preventing people from coming together. Changing is the key.... challenge with an eye towards change is most effective if done with grace and focusing on what works without trashing what came before.

Like - Reply - 12w

Rachele Focardi Best with your book.... Sincerely

Like - Reply - 12w

Rachele Focardi I am looking to talk to a few more BB leaders and would love to have a chat with you if you have time.

Like - Reply - 12w

Rachele Focardi would be a pleasure

Like - Reply - 12w

Rachele Focardi sent you pm

Like - Reply - 12w

Rachele Focardi will look for it

Like - Reply - 12w

Figure 29

Chapter 18

Benefits of Harmonizing a Multigenerational Workforce and What You Risk if You Don't

You can now imagine how the differences, misunderstandings and insecurities I have discussed in the previous chapters can trigger toxic dynamics that prevent organizations from harnessing the power of their human capital. What conflicts can you expect and what can happen if they are not addressed?

I have asked 250 HR professionals what challenges they have witnessed in their organizations as a result of intergenerational differences. You can see their top answers in Figure 30.

WORKFORCE PROBLEMS CAUSED BY INTERGENERATIONAL CONFLICTS

- Discord amongst workers
- Unhealthy competition
- Lack of mutual respect
- Low employee engagement
- High staff turnover and attrition
- Misalignment
- Slow moving projects
- Stagnated innovation
- Slow technology adoption
- Lack of teamwork

Figure 30

This shows that it is not only workforce collaboration to be negatively affected by intergenerational discord, but also

1. The ability to hire the right talent
2. The ability to retain the right talent
3. The ability to drive innovation
4. The ability to build a strong Employer Brand

Let's look at these one by one.

1. THE ABILITY TO HIRE THE RIGHT TALENT

Hiring Criteria

Often times, organizations significantly limit their talent pool because hiring managers are overly fixated on school, degree and grade point average. The new generations are very prolific in their abilities, success today looks different than what it used to, and the skills employers need most go beyond traditional hiring criteria. If hiring managers do not understand this, they are likely to dismiss a great candidate for the wrong reasons. This is one of the biggest frustrations HR professionals have shared with me. *"Most of the times when I put the CV of a great candidate in front of senior leaders, the first thing they look at is the school. If it's not the crème-de-la-crème or their Alma Mater, they won't go any further and will just toss that candidate aside. We miss out on so many great people that way,"* the Head of HR for a **Financial Services Company** shared with me.

Recruiting today is not about settling for a candidate based solely on grades or educational achievements, nor is it about choosing an employer based solely on company prestige. It is about finding the best possible fit between the candidate's personality and the company culture. Organizations should therefore broaden their pool; especially since, with hiring moving to digital, the cost of scale to target based on new criteria — such as interests — or based on school and major, is virtually the same.

Interview Process

While "authenticity" is the word nowadays, it is not always rewarded, especially during the interview process. If interviewers are not up-to-speed with the times and are overtly structured in their approach, or if they get turned off by a candidate's painted nails, unconventional haircuts, or questions about work–life balance, they are likely to reject great talent simply because they behave in a way that is different from what they were once taught was acceptable. *"Interviewers often display bias from the very beginning of an interview just because candidates 'don't act professionally enough', 'don't dress conservatively enough', 'appear too comfortable', or 'ask too many questions about the work culture'. Not only do we lose good people, but we also have to deal with the impact this has on our external brand when candidates share their negative experiences with their peers or online,"* the Head of HR for a **Professional Services Firm** shared with me.

If organizations really value authenticity, they need to ensure this is reflected in the entire candidate-experience. The interview process must feel like a genuine conversation where candidates are not discriminated for being themselves. Taking it as an opportunity to assess talent based on cultural fit is key, and the outcome is win-win. Candidates who do not complement the culture of the organization will be spared from taking a job that is not right for them, while still appreciating the high-touch approach. While those who are aligned with the culture of the organization will know exactly what they are walking into. This ultimately leads to higher offer acceptance, lower cost per hire, stronger engagement, better retention, more productive employees, and a happier work environment.

Compensation

Perks and benefits are more important these days than they ever were with previous generations. Candidates want extended paid leave, remote work, and health, wellness and family-friendly benefits as part of their compensation. If Compensation and Benefits professionals are out of touch with the priorities of each generations, they will not be able to design packages to meet their different needs. Organizations that structure compensation by generations — like **Maybank** — or by life-stage within the generation (accounting for changes in priorities, for example, between someone who is just out of school, and someone who is looking to start a family) — like **Pacnet** did — are much more likely to have their offers accepted. *"There have been so many times when we send the offer letter to young candidates and they get back to us — short of saying 'Is this it?' — asking so many questions about perks that other employers offer and we don't. The compensation team resists these demands, calling the candidates entitled and ungrateful, but this is the way things are now. We need to get onboard!"* the Head of HR for an **Engineering Manufacturing Company** told me.

With talent willing to take a lower base salary in exchange for other perks, organizations that get creative with their compensation packages will not only strengthen their Employer Brand, but also save on salary and decrease attrition.

2. THE ABILITY TO RETAIN THE RIGHT TALENT

Workplace Dissatisfaction

Young generations want to be empowered and recognized. They expect their leaders and managers to provide them with career development opportunities, a clear growth trajectory, and the chance to make significant contributions. While older managers often rely on tenure when it comes to promoting employees or giving them additional responsibilities, Millennials and Gen Z expect and demand much faster progression, which often leads to them bypassing the chain of command. Inability to advance with speed and to drive impact is a big source of friction between young employees and their managers, who struggle with their expectations and their restlessness. *"People who are early in their career get extremely frustrated because they are told they need X years of experience to get promoted, so they leave. We lose good performers this way,"* the HR professional of a **Pharmaceutical Company** said.

If senior employees do not find ways to address this, and young employees do not understand that they also have a responsibility to demonstrate they possess the qualities needed for the success of the business, it will be hard to find a middle ground, and Millennials and Gen Z will leave the organization feeling undervalued.

Lack of Intergenerational Cohesion

While growing up, we are encouraged to spend time with peers from our same age group, and we see older people as either authority figures or vastly different in terms of lifestyle and priorities. Yet, upon entering the workforce, we are expected to collaborate with employees of different ages, whom we barely know or understand. Lack of authenticity, ambiguity, opposing perspectives, and a hierarchical mentality result in lack of cohesion that further intensifies misunderstandings. *"The younger employees tend to stick together. There seems to be little trust between them and the people already in the workplace. It makes informal interaction extremely uncomfortable and this is a pity. At the end of the day, we are all people, and it would be much easier to create a culture of respect, understanding and collaboration, if generations intermingled instead of keeping separate,"* the HR Director of a **Management Consulting Firm** said to me.

Unless organizations invest significant efforts to create bonding experiences for people across age groups, generations will continue to believe they have nothing in common. This will impact their ability to collaborate, which will lead to dissatisfaction and, ultimately, higher turnover.

3. THE ABILITY TO DRIVE INNOVATION

Stagnated Innovation

Intergenerational conflicts drain energy and decrease motivation for fostering innovation. When multigenerational teams are unable to work together, agree on processes and responsibilities and push ideas forward, it may take years for projects to see the light of day.

Millennials and Gen Z have big ideas and are more willing to experiment. However, their solutions and initiatives often fail to get the support of the older generations. *"The biggest challenge we face when it comes to staying ahead of our industry competitors is a top-down approach where key decisions are still made by a specific group of individuals who are not willing to innovate or empower. It is critical that we find sensible ways to 'force' the older generations who remain influential due to their commercial success, to be open-minded and willing to change,"* the Head of HR for an **Advertising Agency** said to me.

This mentality also leads to resistance towards technology adoption, which results in further fragmentation within the business.

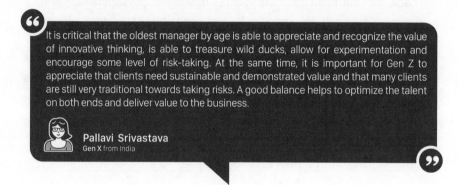

It is critical that the oldest manager by age is able to appreciate and recognize the value of innovative thinking, is able to treasure wild ducks, allow for experimentation and encourage some level of risk-taking. At the same time, it is important for Gen Z to appreciate that clients need sustainable and demonstrated value and that many clients are still very traditional towards taking risks. A good balance helps to optimize the talent on both ends and deliver value to the business.

Pallavi Srivastava
Gen X from India

Figure 31

Diversity = Creativity

Countless studies over the last ten years have proven time and time again that non-homogenous teams where people have different backgrounds, skills, viewpoints, and where everyone has equal voice, result in greater creativity, better outcomes and higher performance. Generational Diversity in a team is fundamental. While Baby Boomers and Gen Z tend to rely on their past experiences, the younger generations want to push new ideas. Both are critically important, and failure to marry the two will significantly impact an organization's ability to drive successful innovation. *"Millennials and Gen Z have great ideas, but often don't know how to scale them because they don't have sufficient knowledge of the industry or experience within the company. It is hard for them to anticipate potential issues. Boomers and Gen X, on the other hand, know exactly how to navigate the organization and are the best at clearing roadblocks when they want to. When these two groups manage to find a way to collaborate, they are unstoppable,"* the Head of HR for a **Biotech Company** said to me.

Inability to Appeal to Consumers

In order for organizations to remain competitive, they need to understand their consumers. This means they must offer products and solutions that appeal to them, and know where and how to engage them. Both on the product development side, and on the marketing and communication side, organizations must give voice to those who understand the consumer segments the best. If the goal is to attract young consumers, Gen Z and Millennials — who are closest in age and mindset — should be the ones to drive product development. Likewise, when the audience is older consumers, Baby Boomers and Gen X should take the lead. The same goes for advertising, as success also depends on the ability to find the most effective way to target and influence the consumer segment. *"I used to work for an organization that wanted to position its product as the n.1 in the market for people age 21-35, but all the decisions were made by senior employees who had no way of relating to the customers they wanted to attract. Yet, probably out of pride, they refused to let the younger teams take over. As you can imagine the product did not sell quite as well as we were hoping,"* a Gen X Marketing Professional said.

The same consideration, of course, must be made when sending young employees to speak to older customers, or vice-versa.

4. THE ABILITY TO BUILD A STRONG EMPLOYER BRAND

And finally, there is the impact that all these negative experiences or unmet expectations have on the company's Employer Brand. In recent years, we have seen a big shift of power from employers to talent. With the vast amount of information available online, talent has a lot more to base their decisions on. Furthermore, they do not only consume data, they also generate content, and they share that content online with virtually unlimited reach. This means that everyone who has had any experience with an organization — as candidate, an employee or a consumer — becomes either an advocate or a critic, and we know that the young generations look upon the experience of peers and influencers when it comes to making important decisions. If they read that a company's culture is unsupportive, that there is lack of collaboration, empowerment, or work–life balance, that the compensation packages are sub-par, or that the candidate experience is unpleasant or biased, they will walk away. In fact, most of the time potential candidates have already made up their mind about an organization and what it is like to work there long before having any direct contact.

LACK OF MULTIGENERATIONAL HARMONY LEADS TO

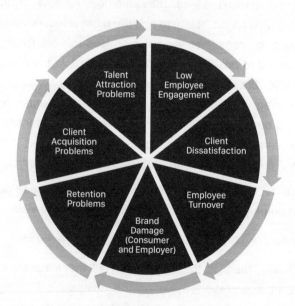

Figure 32

On the other hand, there are significant benefits to be reaped from harmonizing the Multigenerational Workforce. Research has shown that improving employee retention can potentially double a company's revenue growth while significantly increasing the profit margin. Engaged employees have lower turnover rates, higher productivity, and yield to higher profitability. This leads to substantial savings in cost-per-hire, as candidates join an organization for its strong culture and not only for the salary. Finally, a strong, cohesive and collaborative Multigenerational Workforce will have a tremendous impact on the Employer Brand. *Willis Towers Watson Research* shows that companies demonstrating best practices relative to the talent experience are three times more likely to report employees who are highly engaged, and 93 percent more likely to report significantly outperforming their industry peers financially.

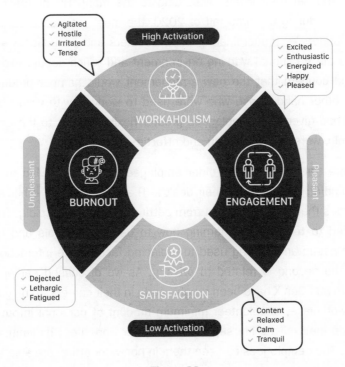

Figure 33

Chapter 19

Covid-19 and the New Normal

Understanding how to lead a collaborative Multigenerational Workforce will be even more critical in a Post Covid-19 world. The varying types of lockdown imposed across the globe made generational differences appear more obvious and discernable. Organizations — forced to conduct split operations and ask their employees to work from home — found themselves having to address the concerns of people across all age groups and seniority levels. According to the many HR professionals I spoke with during the first half of 2020, the most resistance came from senior leaders — predominantly Baby Boomers and early Gen X — who, used to the traditional working environment and office set-up, expressed fear and concern that the new arrangement would hamper productivity. On the other hand, those who were used to working with virtual teams, or who had given their employees greater flexibility prior to the Covid-19 Pandemic, were able to quickly and effortlessly adapt.

The more traditional among older employees, besides having to adjust to not finding their team at their desk at 9 a.m., faced two other sets of challenges that prevented them from getting up to speed rapidly. The first is related to **technology**; learning how to use virtual tools and remote system set-up and getting used to replacing face-to-face interaction with video. The second is related to **privacy**. As we discussed earlier, Baby Boomers and Gen X have been taught, early in their careers, to be guarded in the workplace, to volunteer minimum amount of personal information, and keep their private life separate from their work life. Suddenly, it's on display. Their employees can see them in non-work attire, are able to look into their homes, watch their family members walk by, and for many this represents a major source of discomfort. During virtual meetings, they are likely the ones sitting in front of the same white wall or neutral and well laid-out background wearing more formal clothes.

On the other hand, Millennials and Gen Z are used to sharing their lives on social media platforms. What they do, who they date, where they go, what they eat, what they buy, how they entertain themselves is public knowledge. Edited selfies aside, they do not mind being seen for who they are. They are the ones carrying their laptops around the house during a Zoom meeting as they go into the kitchen, grab a drink, open the front door, walk past a messy living room, or take their children on their laps when they barge in, and introduce them to their co-workers (something that would likely make an older Gen X or Baby Boomer quite uncomfortable — as you may recall from the reaction of Prof. Robert Kelly when his two children walked in on him during a live interview with BBC in 2017).

If we think about it, the comfort level associated with having one's life on display, is a major differentiator across generations. Even movie stars or famous singers nowadays communicate with their audience through video directly from their own home, without any staging, makeup or preparation. This is not something you would see celebrities do in the past, when every appearance was carefully scripted and meant for them to be seen in the best possible light.

Despite the pain, damage and discomfort Covid-19 has brought, it is most likely one of the best things that could have happened from a Multigenerational Workforce point of view. Digitization became imperative for business continuity and survival, and overnight organizations were able to push for the adoption of various communication and collaboration tools. Baby Boomers, with no choice but to adapt, realized that the ability to work virtually, thread work into one's private life, perform multiple unrelated tasks concurrently, and be productive from anywhere, is not only a privilege, but also a skill (and a much needed one, especially in the midst of a Pandemic). At the same time, being outside of their comfort zone and adopting new technologies made senior leaders come across as more human and relatable to their younger employees, creating the foundation for a deeper and more meaningful relationship. In short, the Covid-19 Pandemic "forced" upon older generations the skills they will need in order to continue thriving in the workforce.

Finally, although nobody yet knows what *The Future of Work* will look like, one thing is for certain: HR will not go back to business as usual, and this is likely to become the New Normal. Except this time, it will not only be the younger generations demanding and driving the change, but the older ones as well.

Pressure will come from senior employees who, after months of working from home with no business travel, have had the opportunity to rediscover the value of spending more time with their loved ones. Those who have not been able to fully enjoy family life during most of their career are not likely to give it up again. The second source of pressure will come from the more progressive leaders, the ones who have been connecting well with their teams and peers on a virtual basis well before Covid-19. They will encourage and support even more of their staff to work from home, leading to time and productivity savings from the commute. And then of course, you have Millennials and Gen Z, who have long advocated for more flexibility and who now can present solid evidence that good work can be done from anywhere, anytime.

As a testament to this, in July 2020, **Siemens** communicated a decision to let its employees work from wherever they want for two to three days a week. Deputy CEO and Labor Director of Siemens AG, Roland Busch, said that these changes will be associated with a different leadership style focusing on outcomes versus *presenteeism*. *"The Coronavirus crisis has triggered a surge in digitalization. We've always had mobile working at Siemens, but now we're taking it a step further. The basis for this forward-looking working model is further develop our corporate culture. These changes will be associated with a different leadership style, one that focuses* *on outcomes rather than on time spent at the office,"* Busch explained in a press release dated July 16th 2020. *"We trust our employees and empower them to shape their work themselves so that they can achieve the best possible results. With the new way of working, we're motivating our employees while improving the company's performance capabilities and sharpening Siemens' profile as a flexible and attractive employer."*

In October 2020, **Microsoft** followed suit by announcing its decision to let employees work from home permanently and even consider their requests to relocate to other cities or countries if their work can be done remotely.

While Siemens and Microsoft are two of the first, they will surely not be the last. With Covid-19 accelerating the adoption of digital tools, many organizations will be looking to use this window of opportunity to accelerate digitalization, bringing people together no matter where they are, and making communication less formal.

In addition to flexibility, as the Covid-19 Pandemic unfolded at the start of 2020, the need to show empathy and take care of employees' well-being emerged as a strong imperative for organizations across the world. How people experienced working from home during the various lockdowns varied vastly from person to person, depending on their unique situation.

Those living alone, had more time to devote to work, classes, reading and personal development, but had to face loneliness and isolation. Those in a relationship with no dependents also had more time for themselves, but may have had to face the inevitable challenges that arise when two people have to rely exclusively on one another, without other emotional outlets. On the other hand, those with young children or dependents barely managed their daily workload. Between caring for them, supporting them with home-based learning and ensuring their physical and mental well-being, employees had a hard time adjusting to the new routine and keeping up with their basic daily workload.

All of a sudden there was no standard, and with no guidebook to follow organizations had no choice but to show empathy and flexibility.

Quick to respond, in April 2020 — just days after the start of the Circuit Breaker (Singapore's response to Covid-19) — **DBS** launched its TOGETHER movement, a holistic approach to employee care and engagement. I was extremely impressed by the many initiatives being rolled out in such a short period of time, so I reached out to the company to find out more. During my conversation with Ng Ying Yuan, Chief Operating Officer for Group Human Resources at DBS, I learned that the decision to launch an organization-wide employee movement stemmed from DBS recognizing that some employees may experience anxiety when juggling competing demands for attention as the boundaries between home and the workplace start to blur, and managing these changes to daily routines may not come naturally to everyone. The goal was to keep employees across all age groups and life stages connected and engaged, to encourage mutual care, and to inspire employees to reimagine and create opportunities for growth after Covid-19. Under the movement, DBS rolled out a holistic series of programs around four main themes:

1. **Adopt new behaviours and ways of working**

   With teams operating virtually out of different sites, DBS established new norms to ensure a respectful and productive digital work environment. The company rolled out a communications program containing advice on smoothening the transition to new work arrangements, such as ways to organize work corners at home and suggestions on establishing new work routines. Managers also received guidance on how to better engage their teams remotely, including actionable tips on building team morale, and insights on cultivating trust and empathy from behind the screen.

2. **Build social connections despite new work arrangements**

   In order to prevent the lack of physical meetups or face-to-face conversations from hindering team bonding, DBS introduced new ways for employees to build professional trust. The company encouraged all employees to use its videoconferencing platforms to stay connected socially, and organized virtual team meals and group fitness exercises, as well as "Casual Hangouts" to bring together employees with common interests (such as love for animals, food or charitable work) regardless of their age group. Managers were encouraged to lead the change by introducing new team habits and celebrating positive milestones.

3. **Care for their personal well-being and that of colleagues**

Recognizing that working remotely can take a toll physically and mentally, DBS reminded employees to take charge of their personal health and to nurture a culture of mutual care and concern within the organization. The company distributed care packages comprising surgical masks, hand sanitizers, a thermometer and Vitamin C supplements to all employees. It organized webinars on health and well-being in the context of a Covid-19 world, gave employees free access to a mindfulness application, offered free counselling, and launched a well-being challenge to encourage everyone to take charge of their own physical and mental health.

4. **Use current circumstances as a positive force to develop innovative solutions for the bank, customers and the community**

DBS encouraged employees to see themselves as agents of positive change even during Covid-19 through internal innovation challenges, as well as opportunities for them to contribute to the wider community by distributing complimentary care packages, healthy snacks, lunch bentos, coffee and gelato to healthcare professionals who worked tirelessly in the wake of the Pandemic. Through its SGD 10.5 million "DBS Stronger Together Fund", the bank also empowered its employees to donate meals for the elderly, lower-income households, and migrant workers in Singapore, and amplified their contributions by matching every employee-meal pledge made.

Finally, DBS recognized the need to help employees across all age groups understand how the larger operating environment might impact them, and motivate them to invest in themselves. In April 2020, the bank ran its **LearnShareTeach TOGETHER Festival** to encourage employees across all age groups to adopt digital learning behaviors, pick up new skills, and connect with colleagues through the sharing of knowledge and experiences. And in July 2020, the bank launched its **FutureForward Week**, showcasing a series of webinars and virtual workshops by thought leaders to help employees better understand the megatrends, challenges and opportunities emerging from the new Covid-19 normal, as well as actionable insights on how they can futureproof themselves.

PART 3

Winning Strategies and Initiatives to Harness the Power of Intergenerational Collaboration

"Strategy without Tactics is the slowest route to victory. Tactics without Strategy is the noise before defeat."

Sun Tzu

Introduction

In the previous chapters, we explored why effectively managing a Multigenerational Workforce has become a critical business imperative. We also learned about the forces that shaped each generation, and what contributes to the mutual discord. The next few chapters will cover how to build a culture of Intergenerational Collaboration, and will showcase what leading global organizations are doing to bridge the generational divide.

The very first step to harmonizing the Multigenerational Workforce is to acknowledge and accept these four key points:

First, **Generational Diversity is Diversity**, and although every person is unique, it is also important to recognize that stereotypes exist for a reason and can teach us a lot about ourselves and others. Acknowledging and embracing differences is the only way to harness the power of each generation and build multigenerational teams that can truly drive innovation.

Second, **intergenerational conflicts are very real** — even if employees do not openly talk about them — and if not addressed they will hinder an organization's efforts to create a cohesive, collaborative and productive working environment, affecting client and partner relationships as well.

Third, **frictions between generations stem from a profound lack of contextual knowledge and understanding** of one another. Young employees oppose their managers, and older employees begrudge the young ones because neither of them realizes how strongly the behaviors and the mindsets they disapprove of are rooted in the historical, political and social context that each generation was brought up in.

Finally, when it comes to intergenerational collaboration, five skills are needed above all others: **Perspective-Taking**, **Curiosity**, **Empathy**, **Sensibility** and **Humility**. However, these are seldom taught in schools, and in most organizations little is done to help employees of all age groups acquire these skills. This is unfortunate, because without employees' ability and willingness to take into account different points of view, to understand and share the feelings of others, to be aware of the effect of their behaviors on those around them, and to accept that others are worth listening to, bridging the generational divide effectively is simply impossible.

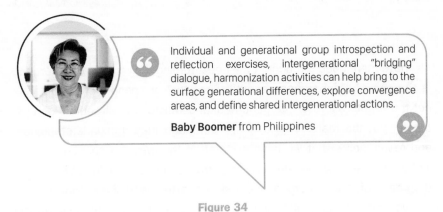

Individual and generational group introspection and reflection exercises, intergenerational "bridging" dialogue, harmonization activities can help bring to the surface generational differences, explore convergence areas, and define shared intergenerational actions.

Baby Boomer from Philippines

Figure 34

There needs to be genuine commitment on the part of the organization to foster a culture of intergenerational collaboration. According to the *2020 XYZ@Work Multigenerational Workforce Study*, while 94 percent of employees across all age-groups believe Generational Diversity is important and should be part of an organization's Diversity and Inclusion agenda, three out of four said their employer shows little or no commitment. This is consistent with only 25 percent of HR professionals saying their organization is strongly committed to Generational Diversity, and 34 percent saying not at all.

Chapter 20

Recognize, Understand, Embrace and Celebrate Generational Diversity

As I have mentioned throughout the book, forcing the attitude of "everyone is the same", "generations shouldn't matter" or "people are people" is not the way to address intergenerational conflicts. Yes, it sounds good *in theory*, but the fears, insecurities, incompatibilities, misunderstandings, and resentments that we have explored in the previous chapters do not just disappear because someone says they do not or should not exist. And they *do* exist, they emerged loud and clear after every single conversation I have had with anybody who has ever worked in a multigenerational environment over the last 20 years. The key to success is not to put the head in the sand, but to address Generational Diversity, call it out, explore it, understand it, get comfortable with it, and then leverage on it.

Prior to Millennials, it was rare for someone to want to openly identify as "diverse." **Diversity** was often seen as a taboo and people feared discrimination. In 2006, I was writing an article about Diversity and Inclusion, and started looking at the responses from a survey of more than 150,000 college students across the U.S.A. and Asia. Two of the initial questions were *"What is your ethnicity?"* and *"What diverse attribute will you bring to your employer?"* The options ranged from diversity of thought or cultural background, to sexual orientation, disability, age, and of course, ethnicity. An overwhelming majority of Gen X respondents chose *"prefer not to say"*, refusing to self-identify with any of the categories provided.

Between 2007 and 2009 all of this changed. When Millennials were the students answering the same questions, they were not only keen to highlight their diverse attributes, but they overwhelmingly requested the ability to select multiple options and provide additional ones. I will never forget when a student answered *"other"* to the ethnicity question and wrote in *"I am an African-American Pan-Australian Jew."* The point is, by openly and fully embracing who they were without fear or stigmas, by viewing their own diverse attributes as a plus and not as a minus, Millennials turned diversity into a strength.

It is time to be just as open and proud about **Generational Diversity**. I keep hearing HR professionals say they do not or cannot use the words "older" or "younger" when talking about generations because they are afraid employees will take offense. But isn't younger or older what generations are? We must remember that the words "young" or "old" only have a negative connotation if we attach one to them. If we accept that it is ok to be "older" and it is ok to be "younger" because both have something utterly unique to bring to the table, then more energy can be spent on appreciating the differences instead of shying away from them.

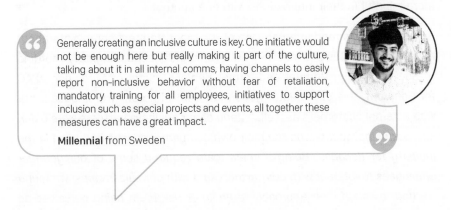

> Generally creating an inclusive culture is key. One initiative would not be enough here but really making it part of the culture, talking about it in all internal comms, having channels to easily report non-inclusive behavior without fear of retaliation, mandatory training for all employees, initiatives to support inclusion such as special projects and events, all together these measures can have a great impact.
>
> **Millennial** from Sweden

Figure 35

The Importance of Cross-Generational Awareness

In the research that I have conducted while writing this book, I asked employees across all age groups what they believe organizations should do in order to address and help resolve intergenerational conflicts. An overwhelming number of them said they would like organizations to find ways to bridge the generational divide through **initiatives that foster curiosity and mutual understanding in a relaxed and informal environment**.

The best way to build cross-generational awareness is to train employees of all age groups on how different generations think, operate and define success. I have run hundreds of sessions for all types of organizations — from large MNCs to smaller family-owned businesses, from traditional industries to tech companies — bringing participants back in time to understand the forces that shaped the behaviors and mindsets of each peer group. What emerged clear as day is that **every generation, one way or another, feels misunderstood**. Leaders can talk about diversity, read all the books about effective leadership styles and conflict management, but will only succeed in harmonizing their Multigenerational Workforce if they provide a platform where the different age groups can openly learn about each other. This will lead to less prejudice and more tolerance; it will help employees not take things personally; and it will encourage them to be more mindful in their interactions with one another.

Being **mindful** is fundamental. One of the most frequent complaints about Millennials and Gen Z is that they are overconfident and haughty. According to Sue Day, Baby Boomer and former Senior Director of Marketing APAC for **Polycom**, this can create friction not only with senior employees, but with external customers as well. "*Many of our business partners were older, successful individuals who ran their own company and who had been in the industry for decades. Being a small team required some of our younger employees to interact with our partners and with our sales teams; we found we had to coach their approach carefully or risk them being perceived as 'cocky youngsters, with limited understanding of the industry, telling more experienced professionals what to do'. As you can imagine, this wouldn't go down well, especially in markets where old age is expected to be revered and honored. It took a lot of work to make our young employees — who come in expecting independence and freedom to express themselves — understand how to interact with older generations, and recognize the importance of nurturing the relationship, building trust, and educating our customers* *on different marketing techniques gently and tactfully."* To address this challenge, Polycom developed a rigorous induction program, where each new joiner was paired with a buddy and coached on how to navigate the organization and communicate with people from different backgrounds inside and outside of the organization.

Sensibility is particularly important for young Millennials and Gen Z when interacting with older generations. From the moment they join the company, weight is given to their opinions, they have direct access to Senior Management, and they are given the opportunity to work on high-impact projects. Most of them have no idea that it took the average Baby Boomer and Gen X years — sometimes decades — before they could make significant contributions to the business or have direct access to company executives. They are also unaware that for the early part of their careers Baby Boomers and Gen X could speak only when spoken to. Without this knowledge, late Millennials and Gen Z will naturally approach senior employees as peers, forthrightly, beaming with confidence and ambition. In many cases, this will rub them off the wrong way, which in turn will reinforce young employees' belief that older generations are resistant to change and are self-important. However, once they become aware that their drive can be intimidating, and that older generations' tough exterior often conceals their fear of becoming obsolete, young employees are more likely to interact with them sensibly and show greater appreciation for their many years of experience.

"Young Boomers were not expected to contribute ideas. Today, everyone is expected to, this is how innovation works. We totally missed that with the Boomers. At the same time, we benefited from a unique economic period. The opportunities we had in our careers were unprecedented, and many Millennials probably feel they won't have the same opportunities. I believe they will and might even have more, but I sense this is an issue with Millennials as it relates to Boomers. If they understood the trade-offs Boomers made (long hours, paying their dues, etc.) to achieve all they did, they might feel differently," Kent, a Baby Boomer, said.

As you can see it is extremely important to help the young generations entering the workforce understand the generational mindset of Baby Boomers and Gen X early on, just as it is critical for the older generations to understand Millennials and Gen Z.

This is why the first step in shaping a collaborative Multigenerational Workforce should always be to **ensure employees** — Baby Boomers, Gen X, Millennials and Gen Z — **understand each other**. An organization should encourage empathy and mutual respect by providing the opportunity for employees to become aware of the reasons and contexts behind pervasive generational behavior, understand the nuances of each generation and capitalize on their strengths. In short, **do not shy away from the elephant in the room**, call it for what it is, address it, laugh about it together, and discuss it until everyone is willing to let down their barriers and start hearing each other out. *"The key is to have some fun. Find a way to get people to talk about themselves without getting too defensive; use anecdotal humor to illustrate comical scenarios of the generational gaps,"* a Gen X from South Africa said.

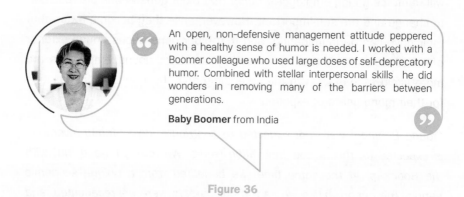

An open, non-defensive management attitude peppered with a healthy sense of humor is needed. I worked with a Boomer colleague who used large doses of self-deprecatory humor. Combined with stellar interpersonal skills he did wonders in removing many of the barriers between generations.

Baby Boomer from India

Figure 36

There are a number of different initiatives — informal and formal — that can help employees across all age groups connect and develop a genuine desire to see the world from each other's perspectives. These include **Generational Awareness Sessions**, **Workshops**, **Coaching Sessions**, **Sharing Platforms**, **CEO and CHRO Roundtables**, **Peer Support Groups**, **Team Bonding Activities**, and **Shared Workspaces**. Whichever the format, the key to success is to ensure the organization cultivates curiosity and non-judgement, offering a safe space where participants can ask questions and share experiences without worrying about hierarchy, office politics or criticism.

Generational Awareness Sessions

If the goal is to create broad awareness across the entire organization, Generational Awareness Sessions where every generation is in the same room work best. They are extremely effective in helping employees become aware of the **key historical**, **socio-economic and cultural aspects** that have conditioned each generation, as well as highlight the **reasons behind the intergenerational conflicts** that currently exist within the workplace. When employees across all age-groups are exposed to the same information at the same time; when every peer group's strengths and weaknesses are exposed; when everyone joins in on the same conversation, what happens is everyone can relate, but nobody feels called out. The outcome is they will be able to look at one another under a new light, feeling more connected, more understood and more understanding.

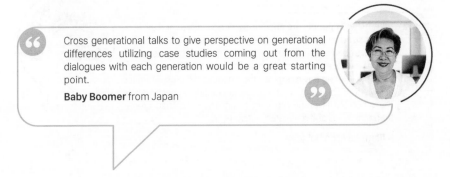

Cross generational talks to give perspective on generational differences utilizing case studies coming out from the dialogues with each generation would be a great starting point.

Baby Boomer from Japan

Figure 37

In 2019, I was running one of these sessions for a large **Private Bank**, addressing both the future leaders of family-owned businesses, as well as bank employees. At the end of the event, I was overwhelmed by the number of Millennials who came up and told me that, for the first time, they understood why their parents or their bosses exhibited certain behaviors. Up until then they thought it was personal, and many were even considering leaving the company or the family business. With a renewed understanding, they were now more than willing to give it another try. Some invited me to run the same session with their parents and their bosses, and months later a dozen of them reached out to let me know that the intergenerational dynamics had changed, and that they were finally able to openly address their differences and build a relationship of mutual respect, understanding and collaboration.

Generational Awareness Sessions can also be run separately for Baby Boomers/Gen X and Millennials/Gen Z. I have seen them work extremely well when there is a new wave of interns or young graduates coming into the organization. In this case, having one session with the line managers (to make sure they understand what to expect from the new joiners and what the new joiners expect from them), and one with the interns and fresh graduates, has been proven to increase significantly the level of satisfaction and engagement throughout the program.

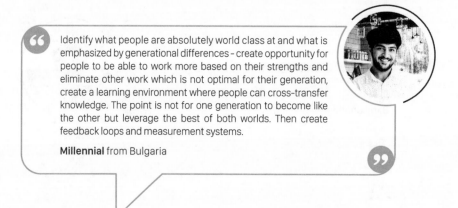

Identify what people are absolutely world class at and what is emphasized by generational differences - create opportunity for people to be able to work more based on their strengths and eliminate other work which is not optimal for their generation, create a learning environment where people can cross-transfer knowledge. The point is not for one generation to become like the other but leverage the best of both worlds. Then create feedback loops and measurement systems.

Millennial from Bulgaria

Figure 38

Workshops

While Generational Awareness Sessions are an effective first step in showing commitment to Generational Diversity, addressing generational differences, and promoting cross-generational understanding, well-facilitated small group sessions where employees from all age groups come together to address their frustrations, their concerns and their desires, are necessary in order to break the cycle and help employees communicate in new, open and honest ways.

Although leaders may worry that compelling employees to directly address intergenerational issues with one another is equivalent to opening a Pandora's Box, if facilitated correctly this confrontation can be extremely fun and productive, and happen in a way that does not offend the participants but brings out humor instead. Workshops provide a "brave space" where employees are able to have a fairly robust discussion without spinning off into arguments. Allowing the conversation to happen in a structured way leads to productive disagreements, productive confrontation and productive idea sparring. The facilitator focuses on identifying the similarities and expanding the perspectives in a structured manner while sensing the group dynamics and ensuring that people do not get stuck.

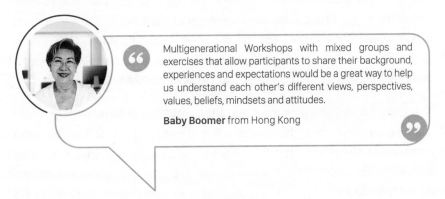

Multigenerational Workshops with mixed groups and exercises that allow participants to share their background, experiences and expectations would be a great way to help us understand each other's different views, perspectives, values, beliefs, mindsets and attitudes.

Baby Boomer from Hong Kong

Figure 39

Managing the process by which people communicate ensures fair and equal participation, so the introverted can contribute effectively without feeling overwhelmed or in the spotlight, and everyone feels empowered to break rank and speak to each other honestly.

Based on my experience with multigenerational groups, **Design Thinking** is the most useful baseline methodology for addressing intergenerational conflicts. The process involves a *Double Diamond* cycle of divergent and convergent thinking around agreed-upon problem and solution statements. Facilitators help participants empathize with one another, discover and prioritize problems, and deep dive and reframe them. They work with a range of visual aids and shared artifacts to structure and guide the conversation encouraging everyone to participate. The shared artifacts act as an anchor, group memory, and an object that moves the conversation from "person-to-person communication" to "group mental model elicitation". This helps people feel they solved a problem and built something collaboratively, escalating commitment along the way.

"In the Multigenerational Workplace, understanding can seem near-frozen, like a sea full of icebergs, with perception blind to the underlying realities. Design Thinking is a human-centered approach asking us to begin with empathy and look below the surface in gaining a shared understanding of problems, to go beyond our habitual ways of thinking and to understand others more deeply. Done right, this is a powerful tool for understanding and action. Organizations that don't get this right are an endangered species," Jon Hoel, principal at Innovator SG and expert facilitator said.

The use of psychometrics tools like **DISC**, **MBTI** or **Gallup** can be a great addition to help identify characteristics besides age that can be used to segment the group, detect similarities of thought and values, or help people better understand, appreciate and tap into the collective strength of each generation. When the workshop is well-facilitated, the immediate outcome is clarity on problems and a great feeling of understanding between participants. However, in order to sustain the benefits of workshops and to keep the momentum, there needs to be a committed program of activities that may include **diagnostics**, **training**, **coaching**, **mentoring** and **additional sessions**.

SAMPLE AGENDA OF A HALF-DAY
MULTIGENERATIONAL WORKSHOP

9 a.m.-10 a.m.	10 a.m.-11 a.m.	11 a.m.-12 p.m.	12 p.m.-1 p.m.
✓ Agenda ✓ Icebreakers ✓ Hopes and fears	Prioritization exercise Which problems should we tackle now/soon/later?	Solutioning exercise: Ideate action pathways to alleviate issues discussed.	Pathways mapping exercise What to commit to doing now/soon/later?
Ideation exercise: What problems do we face? In groups, role play problems from multiple points of view then discuss.	Deep-dive on problems (Levels of Why exercise) **Group discussion:** What are the causes of the problems?	Refine solution statements and examine them against both existing and potential programs of activity.	Discuss potential pathway activities and phases. Discuss immediate steps. Each person commits to do at least one thing differently!

Figure 40

Coaching

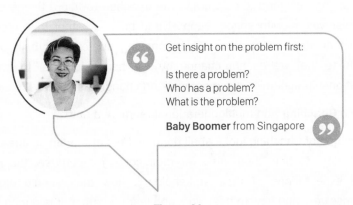

> Get insight on the problem first:
>
> Is there a problem?
> Who has a problem?
> What is the problem?
>
> **Baby Boomer** from Singapore

Figure 41

Coaching is a very effective way to provide support to multigenerational teams. It addresses issues and helps employees reflect and intentionally improve the way they work with each other. *"Teaching (cognitively) can only go so far — especially when, as humans, our emotions regulate our behavior (more than we often care to admit). Coaching is one of the few ways to help people think and feel their way through such growth. Some people do take time to 'reflect' and think that they can do the work they need in private. However, while personal reflection is important for all of us as we work with others, reflection led by the 'why' question rarely results in behavior change that is useful. It mostly leads to firming our own personal biases and judgments about ourselves and others. Coaching can also help us with this,"* Dr. Robyn E Wilson, an experienced individual and team Coach, said to me.

While there are many styles of Coaching to address different situations, the two most beneficial for fostering Intergenerational Collaboration are:

- **Individual Coaching** (one person within the multigenerational team)

  The goal of individual coaching is to support individual employees, helping them face — and sometimes wrestle — their own assumptions, reactions, frustrations, and choices. After ensuring they are psychologically safe (this is critical), the Coach asks relevant open questions designed to encourage the Coachee to figure things out for themselves — with space, support and time — rather than receiving direct advice and opinions. This Coaching approach is built on the premise that we cannot change others, hence in order to improve relationship dynamics, we must work on changing ourselves.

- **Team Coaching** (the multigenerational team as a unit)

  This type of Coaching looks at all the members of a team as one entity, and aims to help them discover their collective purpose, the needs and expectations of their stakeholders, how they should organize themselves, and how to best work and learn together. It is during these sessions that intergenerational conflicts and tensions are most likely to arise, and an experienced Coach is effective in holding the space (and the safety) that enables discussions to flow freely.

"**Steelmanning**" is an effective technique for improving communication and understanding between generations during Team Coaching. This is an empathy exercise where instead of making assumptions about what others are saying and arguing with a distorted, incomplete or inaccurate version of the person's view (aka "**Strawmanning**"), team members are asked to restate what they understand as the person's intended meaning until the person is satisfied that they have been understood. Only then the dialogue can progress. This can take time, but it leads to deeper understanding and helps open up channels of communication.

In order for Team Coaching to be effective, the Team Lead has to be present and participative throughout the entire process. *"While a good Coach can leave an individual or team with tools and processes to help them reassess their development needs and identify new areas of focus to work for continued improvement, success is dependent on having bosses who can continue to coach their teams, and ask good reflection questions. Needless to say, if bosses are perceived to be reluctant to embrace intergenerational differences, displaying instead assumptions and biases and perhaps even demonstrating an ineffectual ability to work across generations, all can be lost quickly. Organizational Culture can make or break all this. After all, things that senior leaders do (or not do) really define the baseline of Organizational Culture,"* Dr. Robyn said.

Sharing Platforms

Sharing is a fundamental requirement for bonding. Employers need to show their commitment to Generational Diversity by providing a platform where employees across all age groups have the opportunity to talk about their experiences, to walk others through their own thinking process, and to ask each other questions in a casual and relaxed environment. During my many conversations and interviews, Gen Z and young Millennials unanimously

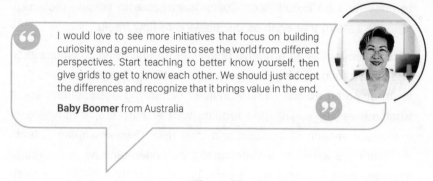

> I would love to see more initiatives that focus on building curiosity and a genuine desire to see the world from different perspectives. Start teaching to better know yourself, then give grids to get to know each other. We should just accept the differences and recognize that it brings value in the end.
>
> **Baby Boomer** from Australia

Figure 42

mentioned their desire to hear from senior employees; particularly stories about their successes, their failures, and other relatable real-life situations. For example, *"When I was your age and I was in your shoes, and I had to make my first sales call, I was utterly terrified!"* Yet, unfortunately this rarely happens in a normal business context. A number of Millennials told me that frequently they do try to reach out to older colleagues with the desire to learn from them and about them, but something in their **body language** makes them come across as "unapproachable". This seems to be particularly common in Asia. *"You know from their face and the way they look at you that they do not want to be bothered. This is a pity because there is so much we would like to ask them about their work and life experience, outside of formal training,"* Nurul, a Millennial from Malaysia working for an **Energy Company**, told me.

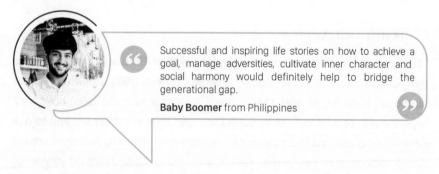

> Successful and inspiring life stories on how to achieve a goal, manage adversities, cultivate inner character and social harmony would definitely help to bridge the generational gap.
>
> **Baby Boomer** from Philippines

Figure 43

The older generations too, have frequently expressed the desire to understand how the young generations think and how they respond to different situations. But since Millennials and Gen Z communicate predominantly through digital channels, senior professionals feel excluded from the new tech-enabled conversations. A shift from siloed to inclusive shared stories and experiences is very effective in addressing this communication gap.

As part of their commitment to embrace diversity in the workplace, **Citi** launched "Generations Network", a global initiative with local chapters run by volunteers from a cross-section of business, functions, nationalities and age groups. The principal focus of "Generations Network" is to promote cross-generational understanding, inclusion, engagement and teamwork. The Hong Kong Chapter, formed in 2016, runs a series of monthly events, both in-person and virtually, meant to foster sharing, curiosity, respect, creativity and empathy.

Some of these events include:

1. **Speed Mentoring** — during this event, 30 young employees (Millennials and Gen Z) have the opportunity to spend three minutes with each of six Managing Directors (Baby Boomers and Gen X) and ask one or more questions related to generational perceptions and realities. After every employee goes around the table, mentees and mentors are asked to share what they learned from one another and what part of the exchange resonated with them the most.

2. **Cross-generational Curated Conversations** — an informal cocktail session where participants are divided into two age groups — 35 and above, and below 35 — and asked to stand at opposite sides of the room. With the help of a moderator, the groups ask each other questions on a variety of topics. For example, Gen X and Baby Boomers explain what it was like to code in the 1980s versus the digital experience in today's world, or talk about what life and work were like before mobile phones existed versus today's smart-phone euphoria.

3. **Storytelling** — a one-hour virtual session to address the importance of being able to articulate one's point of view specifically in the business context. A selected number of participants across different age groups are given one minute to explain what they do in their work. The audience is asked to recite what they did or did not understand, and the presenters then have the opportunity to try and explain what they do again using verbal, non-verbal and a mix of humor until people in the audience receive the message as was intended. This is similar to the Steelman Technique discussed earlier.

Aside from Citi's initiatives above, other effective exercises include **Team Quizzes**, **5-10 Minute "This is Me" Presentations**, **Lunches** where everyone shares personal stories, **Open Face-to-Face "Chit-Chat Groups"** to discuss current events and trends, and **Panels**.

Panels can have two formats. In the first, there are four or five panelists, one from each generation (a Traditionalist and/or a Baby Boomer, a Gen X, a Millennial and a Gen Z) who answer questions from their own perspective (for example, *How would you respond to this situation?* or *How do you feel about X?*). In the second, all panelists belong to the same generation and the questions come from colleagues belonging to other generations (for example, a panel of Baby Boomers and an audience of Gen Z, Millennials and Gen X).

Round Tables and Peer Groups

While informal set-ups are needed to allow different generations to bond, it is also necessary to create more formal forums that provide the opportunity to share difficulties and concerns while building a foundation for collaboration. One highly effective method is to establish regular **CEO or Chief Human Resource Officer (CHRO) Round Tables**. As the name suggests, the Round Table discussion takes place with the participants sitting around a table, taking turns to express their viewpoints regarding the chosen topic. This format is specifically designed to give equal weight to everyone's contribution. It acts as a springboard to a lively and stimulating discussion on best practices, industry trends and any other workplace issues, helping to brainstorm solutions and share valuable knowledge.

Round Tables should be held on a regular scheduled basis, have set themes or topics for the discussion, and be facilitated by a Chair (ideally the CEO and/or CHRO) who has the ability to take action on serious issues and even bring them to the Board. Participants should be people across functions, and include several representatives of each age-group. An ideal mix would be four employees from each of the four generations, each with their own investment in the topic assigned for that Round Table session.

This format opens the discussion to a comprehensive range of different views, as participants both draw on their own individual expertise and share the perspective of the generations they represent. It also has the ongoing advantage of fostering mutual trust. Participants come together on equal terms to brainstorm relevant issues, and benefit from the shared knowledge of the group, while feeling respected and heard.

While Round Tables are dedicated to discussing work-related issues, **Peer Support Groups** provide more personal support and coaching, within the same consistent peer group. Peer Support Group meetings are less structured and formal, with no set theme. They are simply an opportunity to meet with a group of peers and either present a problem or suggest a solution in a safe and trusted environment.

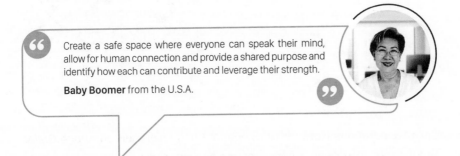

Create a safe space where everyone can speak their mind, allow for human connection and provide a shared purpose and identify how each can contribute and leverage their strength.

Baby Boomer from the U.S.A.

Figure 44

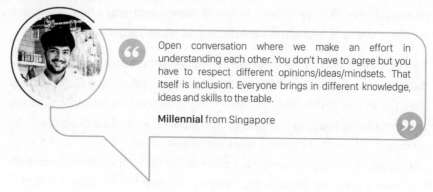

Open conversation where we make an effort in understanding each other. You don't have to agree but you have to respect different opinions/ideas/mindsets. That itself is inclusion. Everyone brings in different knowledge, ideas and skills to the table.

Millennial from Singapore

Figure 45

Team-Bonding Activities

Another fundamental way to bridge the generational gap is to build a strong social network within the organization so employees can foster relationships away from the tension of work-related issues. Joint socials and team activities are a great way to help people of different age groups get more comfortable around each other and build an inclusive community.

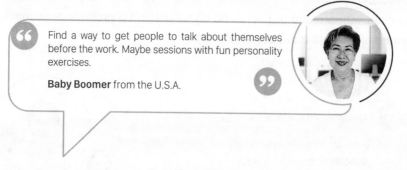

Find a way to get people to talk about themselves before the work. Maybe sessions with fun personality exercises.

Baby Boomer from the U.S.A.

Figure 46

Citi's "Generations Network" in Singapore has leveraged on *Airbnb Online Experiences* to deliver a series of really cool and fun activities as part of their "#best100" work stream, to empower employees to maximize longevity through balance.

These activities include:

- **Mind and Body Masterclass with an Olympic Coach** — a high intensity Zoom workout followed by a sharing session with a former Olympian and current Team U.S.A. Olympic Coach.

- **Workout with a Cirque du Soleil Acrobat** — a Cirque inspired workout followed by behind the scenes Questions and Answers.

- **Happy Hour in Venice** — a live walking tour with a native Venetian guide who can trace his family tree in Venice all the way back to 1576.

- **Coffee Appreciation** — a guided coffee learning and brewing session with a Café CEO and National Coffee Judge.

Other fun bonding activities, aside from the typical team lunches or dinners, are **Bowling** or **Gentle Yoga** (I prefer this over team sports as younger people typically have more stamina and tend to have an upper hand), **Mindfulness** or **Meditation Sessions**, **Virtual Reality**, **Treasure Hunts**, **Karting**, **Karaoke**, **Cooking Classes**, **Trivia Happy Hour**, **Bring Your Parents**, **Bring Your Kids**, or **Bring Your Family to Work Day/Events**, or **Field Trips** and **Off-Sites**.

One of my absolute favorites is **Escape Rooms** with teams made up of one person from each age-group. I particularly like this because team success depends on everyone working together to solve a mystery. Getting out of the room requires different sets of skills and ways of thinking, which means that the different generations have to combine strengths in order to solve the different puzzles in a fun, yet high-pressure environment. Aside from doing wonders in promoting collaboration, there are always some interesting surprises, and a lot that we can learn about our colleagues. You may find out that the person who can see what everyone else missed — and get everybody out! — is the one you would have least expected!

Role-Play is another great way to get people to have fun together, and it has the added benefit of promoting empathy as it helps generations see the world through different eyes. Role-playing a situation from different generations' point of view, for example, generates humor while helping to bridge the generational divide.

Every year, **Procter & Gamble** in China celebrates "Diversity and Inclusion Week" with a number of programs and events to enhance awareness and sensitivity around diversity issues. One of these initiatives is called **Breaking Generational Boundaries**; every participant draws a card with a decade written on it (1960s, 1970s, 1980s, 1990s) and pins it on their shirt. For the rest of the event they interact with each other and role-play different workplace scenarios as if everyone belonged to the generation pinned on their shirt. The goal is to encourage employees to see things from different points of view and to set aside their biases.

Other examples of Role-Play are **"In My Shoes…"** to experience a day as a manager/team lead/decision maker/intern within the organization.

Shared Workspaces

Most people entering the workforce for the first time have limited experience in working within a multigenerational group. The layout of the workplace can either reinforce the inability to connect or overcome it. A traditional workplace has a formal utilitarian set-up, with everyone sitting in their own designated space — seniors in their office, juniors at workstations. This layout does not encourage interaction or collaboration between colleagues. In fact, it can strongly inhibit communication and reinforce generational barriers. A cultural shift has already begun as senior managers are now more committed to a culture of non-hierarchical teams and open-access to leadership. The office layout has changed in response to this shift. Many leaders sit in open offices without glass or partitions these days, demonstrating the open culture they wish to model in the organization. Employees are sometimes allowed to take the shift further, working at standing desks, or on beanbags, with music and whiteboards to stimulate creativity and encourage groupthink.

Establishing a shared workspace may initially come with its challenges — the noise level might rise, and some individuals might be less comfortable with the reduced formality. Despite the initial hiccups, giving employees across age groups the opportunity to sit together, will turn the office into a collaborative space where they can learn from each other and have fun together.

One way to break down barriers is to introduce **food**. Eating together gives people the opportunity to relax and interact more naturally. *"When I first set up my team, everybody around us was very serious, wore a suit, sat in their cubicle while dreaming of a private office, and measured their importance by the number of screens they had. All of a sudden, a bunch of colorful, raggedy, loud people arrived. Brought their own beanbags, standing desks, whiteboards and music, and started working right beside them. At the beginning it raised a lot of eyebrows, but once we started to ship product and bring in results, they loved hanging out in our area, sometimes to learn something new, or to listen to music and eat our candy, or even simply to lighten up their day. Shared workplaces — cross-functional and cross-generational — are important. They create connective tissue and make it easier for people to get used to each other. More often than not, both sides end up enjoying the diversity and opportunity to learn,"* Stephanie, a Millennial engineer who works for an **International Bank**, and who has been given the opportunity to redefine her team's workspace said to me.

Shared workspaces are not just physical, but they are virtual as well, and it is important for employers to explore new ways to improve employee engagement, coordination and communication via various digital tools and initiatives. According to Adrian Tan, Practice Leader at PeopleStrong, reinventing communication tools is critical to bridging the generational gap. *"There are already tons of communication tools in the market. Teams, Slack and many more. Unfortunately, most have learning curves and are not exactly consumer-grade. And with so many new tools entering our lives, few have the patience to read the manuals and play with them. I for one still haven't bothered figuring out how to do a Teams meeting with people outside of my organization. This is where B2B products which mirror typical consumer versions will excel. Workplace by Facebook is a great example as they are similar to the consumer Facebook we are all so accustomed to."*

Organizations must be on the lookout for engaging advanced collaboration technologies to run workshops and conferences, and will need to work on developing relevant capabilities and skills in their employees to ensure they are able to work effectively with new processes and tools.

Chapter 21

Use Collaborative Decision-Making to Create Winning Multigenerational Teams

As companies become more age-diverse, it is important to be proactive about fostering harmony and a shared purpose in teams, and cultivate mutual respect, productivity and innovation. Having the opportunity to work side-by-side in a non-hierarchical, safe and transparent environment that encourages collaborative decision-making, leads to a deeper appreciation and respect for each other's strengths and accumulated wisdom.

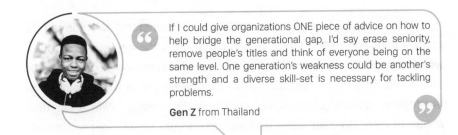

> If I could give organizations ONE piece of advice on how to help bridge the generational gap, I'd say erase seniority, remove people's titles and think of everyone being on the same level. One generation's weakness could be another's strength and a diverse skill-set is necessary for tackling problems.
>
> **Gen Z** from Thailand

Figure 47

A good manager who can liaise between generations will empower all employees through transparent and inclusive leadership. It can be difficult to come across as a fair leader when bringing together people from different age groups, with different expectations and communication styles. The key to success is creating an open-minded and inclusive environment where everybody has a voice. Acknowledging the skills and abilities that each generation can bring to the table and deploying them towards a shared vision will go a long way to making everyone feel valued for their contribution. After all, like in sports, any successful team requires players with different strengths for each position. Next, is to encourage collaborative decision-making while establishing a fair and transparent system of performance evaluation and set goal-oriented work so individuals can see their efforts being recognized. Another valuable strategy is to draw employees together outside of the work environment, so they can foster a team spirit and greater mutual appreciation.

This is how Gonzalo Ruiz Calavera, Head of Global Talent Acquisition for **Siemens** and a Baby Boomer, managed to create a winning multicultural and multigenerational team that brought about disruptive innovation at record speed. During my conversation with Gonzalo, I discovered that he was able to harmonize a group of highly diverse individuals by **Articulating His Vision**, **Having Fun**, **Breaking Boundaries**, **Ensuring Common Understanding**, **Being Agile**, **Leveraging Each Generations' Strength** and **Rewarding Joint Success**.

In 2015, Gonzalo took on the challenge to transform his company's entire Talent Acquisition function globally to meet the needs of the future workforce. He understood that the rise of technology, demographic shifts and tougher competition would require an entire new approach to identifying, recruiting, developing and retaining people. With a big task ahead of him, Gonzalo knew that success would heavily depend on his ability to step away from herd mentality and bring together people who could challenge one another. He needed a multinational, multicultural, multifunctional and multigenerational team if he were to succeed in bringing about real innovation.

Getting employees from different age groups, different nationalities, different cultural backgrounds, and different areas of the business to work together proved to be both painful and rewarding. Gonzalo had to spend the greater part of his time managing the change process to ensure that all moving parts of the ecosystem would fit nicely with one another.

Gonzalo's top priority was to **clearly articulate his vision**. He saw success as the glue holding everyone together, hence he made sure that all individuals within the team understood the role they had to play. "*After all,*" he thought, "*who doesn't want to be successful?*" To Gonzalo, success was not only about reaching the goal, but also about enjoying the ride. Far from being a source of distraction, he knew that incorporating an element of fun would inject positivity and most importantly strengthen the bond between his employees. "*I wanted us to* **have a great time!**" Gonzalo told me. "*We were going to be so disruptive, it had to be a fun experience. So, I chose to focus on our internationality, highlighting the fun elements of working in a cross-cultural setting. Food was a big one. We made it a point to try all types of food. When we traveled overseas, the colleagues in the host country would proudly organize sightseeing trips and introduce the rest of us to their local culture and cuisine. It turned out to be a wonderful team-building activity.*"

But having people from different cultures and age groups come together, inevitably caused a series of misunderstandings that could not be addressed simply by having fun together. Gonzalo found himself having to spend a lot of time and energy helping his employees understand each other. "*One of the main things I observed, particularly between different generations, is that what people say is rarely received in the way it's intended. We'd be in a meeting where someone was explaining something, and the rest of the team would understand something completely different. I was amazed at how frequently a basic message ended up being decoded incorrectly,*" Gonzalo said. In order to avoid this pitfall, Gonzalo requested that all members of his team ask clarifying questions after someone shared or explained something, to ensure they understood correctly. To his dismay, 50 percent of the time, the message was not received as intended, especially by employees belonging to different age-groups. Making it a habit to **seek clarification** went a long way in helping Gonzalo's team reach full alignment and bring about effective outcomes to problems and projects.

The next challenge for Gonzalo was getting people to take initiative and work together to define the best way forward. "*I had to spend a lot of time explaining to my team that I didn't want to be constantly asked for direction. I told them that I would be asking questions, but I was not going to tell them what to do. I wanted them to understand that it had to be a co-creation effort."* In order to encourage his team members to jointly come up with solutions instead of getting into competition with one another, Gonzalo engaged an external Coach. *"Initially, I tried to coach them directly myself, but they saw me as the one who measures performance and promotes people, so they would spend the entire time trying to prove to me that they were right in their way of thinking or in the way they planned to execute the project. I needed them to understand that there was no right or wrong way, but we would have to decide together what 'right' or 'wrong' meant by bringing everyone's perspective into the game."*

The sessions with the external Coach had the added benefit of becoming a platform where employees could emotionally dump all their frustrations. After a while, they **opened up**, showing their own vulnerabilities, understanding their teammates', and interacting with one another in an authentic way. *"Since the beginning, I had encouraged my team to openly address the elephant in the room. Only when they realized it was OK to be themselves, they were finally ready to listen to each other and work together."*

Finally, Gonzalo had to dismantle the traditional, rigid, hierarchical and industrial way of working, in favor of a more **innovative and agile** one. This proved to be particularly difficult for the older generations. People with many years of experience tend to be process-oriented. They approach project structure in a sequential manner. Younger people, on the other hand, are comfortable with parallel processing and multitasking. With only one year to complete the task, Gonzalo needed to make the best use of everyone's strengths; he relied on the youngest generations to **come up with innovative ways to get things done**, and on his most senior employees to **execute on those strategies leveraging their knowledge of the organization and their connections**. After only a few months, older employees started welcoming any opportunity to work with the younger ones, and vice-versa. *"It was transformative to watch them rely on each* *other. The younger employees came up with fresh, simple ideas, used technology effectively and had no constraints in their thinking. The older employees had a better understanding of the challenges of the organization and could use their knowledge to help find solutions. They were all competent in their own areas of responsibility, and when they understood that the way to manage the project was not to define what had to be done in a process sequence, but how to solve problems to make it happen, they started relying on each other's expertise rather than age. That's when the magic happened!"*

Throughout the entire process, Gonzalo stressed the importance of **joint success**, putting significant emphasis on shared progress and rewarding each and every milestone, not only through dinners or internal social media posts, but by working directly with HR to create awards showcasing how collaboration led to success. Everyone felt proud of being a part of the team and — no matter whether they were young or senior employees — everyone felt recognized.

Gonzalo tapped into diversity and provided an environment where every employee felt safe and free to share not only their ideas but also their concerns. He encouraged his team to discover synergies by experimenting together.

Every manager and team leader can harness the strengths of different generations by replicating Gonzalo's multigenerational diverse team model on a smaller scale. This can be achieved by **creating a list of important projects connected to higher level strategy, removing seniority, giving everyone a common goal** and the **opportunity to make their own unique contribution**, and **giving the team visibility within the broader organization**. The benefit of shared projects is that everyone works towards the same goal, and tasks are broken down so everyone is an expert at something and comes in with an equal voice.

Chapter 22

Shift the Mindset of Your Senior Leaders

"One's mind, once stretched by a new idea, never regains its original dimension."

— *Oliver Wendell Holmes Sr.*

Gonzalo is a natural team leader, he is inspired, inspiring, relates well with younger generations, and uses his authority to empower. With talent development hot on every organization's agenda, many senior employees feel the pressure to suddenly transform and adhere to this new standard of leadership and people management. But frankly, until recently, leaders were not expected to "care" about their employees — not in the way they are expected to today. When Baby Boomers and Gen X dominated the workforce, a leader was someone who commanded a group, and being nice was not part of the job description.

This applied to nearly all authority figures. Just think about teachers and school principals. They may have been friendly, empathetic and humorous outside of work, but among their pupils they were strict and intimidating. It is only with Millennials that a leader became someone whose role is to **inspire**, **empower** and **develop**.

Employers will set their most senior employees up for failure if they put them in charge of managing the young generations without having a deep understanding of why a strong and healthy manager–employee relationship is important for the organization, and what it takes to build one. Most employers address this need by offering leadership skills training, and while mastering the art of negotiation, influence and conflict management is important, it is simply not enough. The first step — and the most critical one — should be to **encourage and facilitate a change in mindset**.

> Great leaders are the ones who are willing to adjust their mindset first. Only after that happens, they can truly understand and motivate the people they are to lead.
>
> **Gen Z** from Indonesia

Figure 48

Let's put ourselves in the shoes of today's most senior leaders for a moment. For a large part of their working lives, they were told to exert authority, to be detached, to demand from their employees reverent and subservient behavior. All of a sudden, as they approach the end of their careers, they are expected to become amicable, encouraging, compassionate, attentive, communicative, and to spend a large part of their work-week mentoring and coaching their employees (who are now no longer regarded as subordinates, but equally valuable members of the organization). This requires challenging the very notion of "manager" they experienced throughout most of their careers, and to excel in areas they received no training in and most likely had no role models to learn from. Now, if we put aside the fact that many people are not empathetic or caring by nature, even those who are, had to suppress this inclination for decades while on the job. This is why it is so important, first and foremost, to make senior leaders understand that it is okay to let down their guard, and help them get comfortable with this new concept of leadership.

A leading Asian organization that asked to remain anonymous, recently launched two separate initiatives as part of their signature leadership program in an effort to support the most senior employees with this mindset shift. The first is an *Ikigai* **Workshop**. For those who are not familiar, *Ikigai* is a Japanese concept that means *"a reason for being"* and refers to having a direction or purpose that makes life worthwhile. During the session, senior employees were encouraged to look for meaning in their life and in their work.

In the last few years, there has been a lot of focus and emphasis on the importance of having a purpose, and the young generations now view it as the key to professional achievement. However, the approach of Baby Boomers or Gen X to their careers was pragmatic. Work was not meant to be enjoyable, it was simply a transaction, they did what they had to do to provide for their family and support their lifestyle. People who followed a less conventional path and talked about finding their mission in life were mostly ridiculed, called hippies, unambitious, feeble or inept. I remember a career advisor telling me once when I was a student that people who love what they do are those with a hobby — not a job.

According to the company representative, what started as an experiment quickly became an invaluable and emotionally charged event. Most participants had not asked themselves *"What is my mission in life?"* before, and many realized they had no immediate answer. But as the day progressed and they became more comfortable, interesting things emerged. The *Ikigai* initiative helped participants understand two critical things. First, a great leader today is one who helps employees find meaning in their work — or even better, **supports their need to connect work to their purpose in life**. Second, a manager who never thought about Purpose as important for themselves, cannot possibly think of it as important for the rest of the team. As human beings, we all have this innate and deep-rooted need to feel there is meaning in our life, but sadly, most Baby Boomers and Gen X grew up without paying any attention to it and being told it is not important. What the organization achieved with the *Ikigai* event was to ignite that powerful force each of us innately possesses, helping its senior leaders understand themselves more deeply so they can better understand their people.

The second initiative focused on the notion of **Energy Management**. For most of their careers, Baby Boomers and Gen X were told to get things done, no matter what they had to sacrifice in the process. Leaders often work late nights and on weekends at the expense of sleep, exercise, family and personal downtime. Because this is all they know, they often expect the same from their employees, which sadly makes them appear insensible and uncaring, and contributes to the discord between generations.

The program was introduced to draw attention to the importance of *physical, emotional, psychological and spiritual wellness.* It aimed to help leaders understand that their approach to work is not healthy or sustainable. Because of the way they were raised and the pressure they put on themselves, older generations have a strong sense of duty and believe that their team expects them to be the first ones in the office and the last ones to leave. They do not understand that in order to find the energy to look after the growing demands of their team, **they have to become more sensitive to their own needs**.

Bridging the gap between generations must start with the belief that all employees, regardless of age, have an innate need to find purpose and balance in their life. Sadly, most Baby Boomers and Gen X grew up with the skewed notion that these things are not important (mental health issues, for example, were considered a taboo and were not to be spoken of) and this prevents them from connecting with the new generations.

If leaders have a purpose and find meaning in what they do, they will affect their entire team. If leaders have high energy and manage it well through nutrition, sleep and balance between work and life, they will wish the same for their employees.

Senior managers are often strict to their own traditions even if they are not healthy, and they expect the same from young people.

Gen Z from Philippines

Vs

Millennials and **Gen Z** have learned the importance of taking care of themselves, being healthy, enjoying life and doing what makes them happy. This is something we should learn. It's never too late!

Baby Boomer from the U.S.A.

Figure 49

Chapter 23

Don't Underestimate the Importance of Manager–Employee Relationships

> *"An employee's motivation is a direct result of the sum of interactions with his or her manager."*
>
> — ***Bob Nelson***

The main source of intergenerational conflicts stems from a strained relationship between young talent and their managers. Millennials and Gen Z often feel that old-school management styles, limited understanding of technology (and the organizational structures it enables), and the inability of older managers to connect with them, slow down their career prospects, and prevent them from making significant contributions.

Yet, the single biggest mistake I have seen organizations make — over and over again — is placing the wrong people in management positions. Let's face it, not everyone has what it takes to effectively manage people, not by today's standards. Years of experience are not enough, and industry knowledge alone does not automatically qualify someone to lead a team, especially a multigenerational one. The reality is, we are not all people-persons, not everyone has Gonzalo's innate ability to understand and nurture young employees, and many great contributors simply do not have the disposition, the aptitude or even the interest to manage and develop others. And here's the thing: **that's OK!**

Unfortunately, few will admit to it for fear that it will negatively impact their career, and accept roles that are not fit for them and, often times, they do not enjoy. Naturally, this causes damage on multiple fronts: experienced employees — set up for failure — are distracted from doing what they are best at, and feeling inept in their new mandate, lose interest and motivation. Young employees — attracted by the promise of inspiring leaders who will support their development — feel cheated and leave. The organization ends up losing both the senior individual contributors and the high-potential young talent. At the same time, the failed experience reinforces the mutual distrust and veiled resentment between the generations, and to top it off, the Employer Brand takes a massive hit.

The successful pairing of manager and employee is a delicate process, one that requires time and careful consideration. It is not just about shared goals, objectives and expertise, but common interests, values, rituals and complementing communication styles.

Identifying the right person to lead a team is particularly critical when there is a change in the reporting structure. A few years ago, Alexandra, an engineer who had spent most of her working life building tech startups, was approached by a large **Telco Company** looking to set up a venture builder studio. She had no interest in taking a corporate job, but the organization seemed to understand the importance of driving innovation and thus promised an environment where an engineer — particularly one with an entrepreneurial background — could make significant contributions. So, after much deliberation, she decided to join. Her concern that the environment would be overly traditional and bureaucratic was soon put to rest. The organization was open to embracing new ideas, she was able to hire her own team of engineers and manage them agilely and informally, and was even given a budget to transform her office environment to be more creative and "Millennial-friendly". But what made her experience exceptional was the relationship she had from day one with her direct manager — a Gen X — and her business sponsor — a Baby Boomer. Despite working all of their careers in traditional industries, they were surprisingly "unconventional". They welcomed the start-up mentality and actively promoted it across the business. They aligned the team behind a shared vision and empowered them to take ownership of it. They helped her navigate the organization, and encouraged upward communication, giving her plenty of visibility among Senior Management across the wider organization. Most importantly, they made Alexandra feel she was working on her own startup, and they allowed her to run it that way. As a result, within a short period of time, her unit was globally showcased as an example of performance, innovation and progress.

Sadly, after two years her manager was promoted and replaced by someone who had spent his entire career within a more traditional branch of the organization, and who had no experience in leading tech teams or working with startups. From one day to the next, without any warning, Alexandra's experience with the company changed dramatically. Not only was his management style highly hierarchical and controlling, but her new manager also had little understanding of the formal and informal governance models within the team, what motivated and incentivized them, and what stakeholder networks operated in the background.

The young generation, especially engineers and entrepreneurs, have a need to own their work. They take risks and work extra hard, so they can create an impact and be recognized for it. Needless to say, going from an environment where every opinion mattered, where everyone worked collaboratively to define the vision, the product and the best way forward, to being told *"It's my job to decide what is to be done and it's your job to do what I say to make it happen,"* was extremely demotivating. Furthermore, in an effort to exert greater control, the new manager forbade skip-level communication. With all the hard work and passion Alexandra and her team put into their job, it was extremely important for them to be able to discuss their work freely within the organization. Instead, they were told *"When it comes to Senior Management, I am your mouthpiece, I represent your work."*

Within weeks, the reality of a corporate job suddenly kicked in. Alexandra became demotivated, productivity took a toll, and the dynamics within the team started changing. *"Under the previous manager there was a strong sense of belonging; everyone took more pain and discomfort than necessary to make things happen, but the sense of ownership and recognition we received at all layers of the organization made it worthwhile,"* Alexandra told me. *"With that gone, everyone in the team simply stopped caring."*

Alexandra tried to address her concerns with her manager, but instead of welcoming the feedback and seeing it as an opportunity to build an improved relationship with his new team, he acted defensively and took it personally. This made Alexandra's interaction with him even more uncomfortable and dysfunctional. Without the ability to reach out directly to Senior Management (as this was now frowned upon) she accepted another offer and left the company. Within months, most of the engineers she was able to bring into the organization under the promise of a startup environment also left, and three years of progress were wiped out. Furthermore, the organization struggled to attract and retain talent with the skills necessary to continue to build on what Alexandra and her team had accomplished.

IDENTIFYING
PEOPLE LEADERS

1. Encourage people to be honest about their interest in leading people and teams, and let them know it's OK if it is not their calling.

2. Identify those who have real passion and disposition for developing people and make them accountable for the success of those they manage.

3. Personality matters, so pay careful attention to who you choose to lead a particular group of people, ensuring understanding of team dynamics and synergy.

4. Define leadership as a teachable skill. Train and coach those who may not have strong management skills but do have a genuine interest in people.

5. Don't oust those who don't, instead leverage their deep expertise and knowledge where they can create value. i.e. give them a Figurehead role instead of a Leadership role.

6. Ensure that whether an employee has a Figurehead or Leadership role, the value of their contribution and skills are widely communicated and aknowledged.

Figure 50

Chapter 24

Choose Your Leaders Wisely and Hold Them Accountable

"The conventional definition of management is getting work done through people, but real management is developing people through their work."

— *Agha Hasan Abedi*

We all heard the saying *"People don't leave companies; they leave their managers,"* and this is exactly what happened with Alexandra. So, what went wrong and how can an organization avoid such pitfalls?

While writing this book, I came across a blog titled *"The Right Manager."* The author, Nathan Broslawsky, is an engineer by background who shares my passion for helping organizations build and lead successful teams, so I decided to reach out to him. According to Nathan, any change in reporting structure should be done thoughtfully, infrequently and consensually. *"Simply put: for organizations to truly recognize and embrace the need to develop their leaders, the heads of these organizations must define and articulate the reasoning behind why certain individuals report to others. These individuals in positions of organizational authority need to be very intentional about balancing the needs of the business with the strength and permanence of the relationship between employees and their managers. The decision to pair an employee with a manager should not simply be a by-product of organizational structure: it should be a deliberate representation of the management ethos across the company."*

In Alexandra's case, the organization's first mistake was **underestimating the importance of finding the right manager**; the second was **failing to acknowledge the potential implications** and **openly discuss the change**; the third was **not putting the proper processes in place to evaluate whether the manager–employee pairing was a successful one**. Lastly, it was **allowing great talent to walk out the door** instead of finding ways to remedy the situation.

According to Nathan, periodic skip-level one-on-ones between an employee and the manager's boss during the first 90 days would have provided an ideal platform to understand how the new manager–employee relationship was developing. In Alexandra's case it would have also given Senior Management the opportunity to notice, discuss and address her change in behavior and motivation, likely preventing her from walking out the door.

Finally, Nathan mentioned one more thing that I think is extremely important to highlight. When the manager–employee relationship does not work, it should not reflect poorly on either the employee or the manager. Instead, it should simply be an indication that the pairing between the two was made with imperfect and incomplete information.

I have been advocating this for a long time: if organizations become more thoughtful in the way they bring people together, and are open about the inevitable fact that — even with the best intent — not every manager will be able to get the best out of every employee, there will be no stigma when things do not work out. Instead both the employee and the manager will be incentivized to openly discuss the challenges in the relationship and suggest or accept changes, if necessary. Finally, let's not forget that, despite the many expectations set upon the managers to develop others, they themselves are employees who in turn need to be developed.

Let us look at a company that has been known to place a lot of emphasis on the individual connection between line managers and each young hire, as well as to provide managers with extensive resources, support, and training. What makes **Procter & Gamble** best-in-class when it comes to people management is a strong focus on **Accountability**, **Open Dialogue**, **Internal Promotion Matrix** and **Individual Coaching**.

Managers are evaluated on how they grow the organization, develop people and plan for succession. Unlike many organizations where upward communication is discouraged or scrutinized, at Procter & Gamble, there is a strong emphasis on growing talent from within, and a "Straight Talk" culture that encourages young talent to have a direct line of communication to Senior Management. In addition, all employees have a chance to provide annual upward feedback on various aspects of their line managers' coaching and daily leadership. On one hand, this allows Senior Management to always be in-the-know about what is going on at different layers of the organization. On the other hand, knowing that their team members have regular opportunities to share their experience directly with their boss, motivates managers to have an ongoing open dialogue with their employees. This allows them to be aware of any issues or concerns, and work promptly and collaboratively to resolve them.

Furthermore, managers' promotion is directly linked to the impact they have on the organization through the people they have in their care. This is crucial, as the higher employees progress in corporate hierarchy, the more important it becomes for them to **exhibit impactful leadership**, **build followership**, and **positively engage and influence**. In order to help build Manager's Accountability and People Management skills, all managers are evaluated through an **annual upward feedback cycle**. This mirrors various aspects of People Management — from Coaching to Priority Setting and Engagement — with individual employees and teams. Managers discuss the outcome with their own managers, who then create an individual development plan to help them overcome challenges and limitations, and improve their impact as a leader.

Google is another great example of an organization that has a strong commitment towards developing leaders. Employees are periodically asked to evaluate their managers based on 13 questions. You can see the full list of **Google Leadership Evaluation Questions** in Figure 51.

GOOGLE LEADERSHIP
EVALUATION QUESTIONS

① My manager gives me actionable feedback that helps me improve my performance

② My manager does not "micromanage" (get involved in details that should be handled at other levels)

③ My manager shows consideration for me as a person

④ The actions of my manager show that he/she values the perspective I bring to the team, even if different than his/her own

⑤ My manager keeps the team focused on our priority results/deliverables

⑥ My manager regularly shares relevant information from his/her manager and senior leaders

⑦ My manager had a meaningful discussion with me about career development in the past 6 months

⑧ My manager communicates clear goals for our team

⑨ My manager has the technical expertise required to effectively manage me

⑩ I would recommend my manager to other Googlers

⑪ I am satisfied with my manager's overall performance as a manager

⑫ What would you recommend your manager keep doing?

⑬ What would you have your manager change?

Figure 51

Unfortunately, unlike Procter & Gamble and Google, not all employers have such strong processes and systems in place to ensure and track manager–employee satisfaction across all layers of the organization, and most underestimate the negative impact that choosing the wrong leaders can have on the business.

A manager–employee mismatch affects the entire team. Research has shown that when managers do not feel accepted by their subordinates, their stress levels increase, and they tend to overtly emphasize their own experience when managing employees. This further escalates discontent among young team members who prefer managers who display intellectual ability and knowledge. At the same time, conflicts with their boss lead to feelings of ambiguity within the team. Millennials and Gen Z have strong need for closure, and when it is not met, they are more likely to use self-promotion tactics to inflate their achievements and abilities in order to impress their leaders. This has an adverse effect on the relationship with peers, which in turn negatively impacts both motivation within the team and job performance.

While personality and cultural compatibility are critical, choosing a boss who can align his management style to the needs of his employees is just as important. According to Dr. Rajeev Chib, expert in organizational leadership focused on generational motivations and behaviors "*Millennials and Gen Z respond best to encouraging management styles, such as* **Guidance Coaching***, more directive in nature, and* **Facilitation Coaching** *where they 'learn by doing'. These preferences however vary between age groups, so it is critical for organizations to train managers on the different coaching styles and their unique impact on different generations' job performance.*"

This means that there is a strong need to improve recruitment efforts and have a good mix of people in Senior Management who understand and promote the importance of people management in a multigenerational workplace.

Chapter 25

Prepare the Young Generation for Leadership

In December 2019, I was invited to attend the *In Conversation with Barack Obama* event organized in Singapore by The Growth Faculty. One of the things that resonated with me the most was Obama's take on **Future Leadership**. The former U.S. President attributed many of the world's problems to old people — usually old men — not getting out of the way and not allowing young leaders to take their place. *"Even if I could stay for a third term, I still would not do it. I believe in renewal of leadership and that old people should get away. If people with old ideas stay, new ideas are squashed, and tragedies come from that impulse [to stay in power]. It's time for new ideas, new legs,"* Obama said. Naturally, he was talking about leadership from a political standpoint, but this does hold true not only when running countries, but when running organizations as well. If success is defined by what a leader does to promote business sustainability, one of the most important contributions anyone can make is **preparing the new generation for leadership**.

With Millennials taking on more and more roles in Senior Management positions — and an entire new generation on its way into the workforce — mentoring and developing future leaders will have to become a top priority for every organization. The leaders of tomorrow will have to face a whole new set of challenges and will require a whole new set of skills in order to thrive in The Fourth Industrial Revolution, particularly in a post-Covid world. Being able to identify managers with both vision for the future and a strong generational mindset to support them along this journey will be particularly important. Especially because older generations will have to prepare the new generations for challenges that they themselves never had to face.

Don't Mold Them — Help Them Uncover Their True Potentials

When Baby Boomers were fresh into the workplace, preparing a young person for leadership was fairly simple: it meant molding them to one's own image. Young people-in-training were expected to follow, observe and replicate. There was a set of criteria that someone had to satisfy in order to progress. While there was an emphasis on continuous learning, the bulk of the exposure was through direct working experience and, particularly, through testing of one's capabilities across various situations. *"I always felt that I was constantly being assessed, formally and informally, and that the more I behaved in accordance to the expectations of my 'mentor', the better chances I had to advance. The closer I resembled my mentor's style of leadership, the greater the chances I would be promoted. Respect and reverence were important facilitators for success. Hard work, persistence and the capacity to take on even the most difficult challenges were critical in securing and sustaining sponsorship by your 'mentor'. I specifically used the word 'sponsorship' and not 'mentorship', as the relationship, in my view, had always been one of benefactor-to-beneficiary. In order to qualify as a 'beneficiary', you had to prove your worth regularly. This could only be achieved through alignment and absolute compliance,"* Stephen Tjoa, Baby Boomer and Senior Partner at KPMG Singapore, said.

Young talent today would not settle for a "benefactor–beneficiary" type of relationship. They want to work alongside leaders who can **inspire** them, who are **authentic**, whom they can **relate to**, who can leverage their unique attributes to help them **unlock their true potential** and become leaders of the future. There is no better example to illustrate this point than an experience I had in 2016, when I was invited by **Unilever**'s Regional Leadership and Organization Development Director to talk about the importance of harmonizing the Multigenerational Workforce at *UFLP Connect* in Singapore, an event to welcome all the students who were selected across Southeast Asia and Australasia to join the **Unilever Future Leaders Programme**. What is unique about this particular program is that it is specifically designed to develop Unilever's Future Leaders by accelerating their readiness to take on business leadership roles through rotations within and across functions, impactful projects and extended leadership contact.

As I observed this high potential group of youngsters from the stage, I could not help but think how much things have changed since I was fresh out of school. They were barely in their 20s, and yet this entire event was about them and *for* them, with senior leaders there to welcome them as they embarked on an incredible learning journey with one of the best employers in the world. The first thing I noticed, was how much color was in the room. Forget the black or dark blue suit and white shirt that everyone — except the few who were brave enough to be different — would have worn back in my day. Everyone was dressed informally, according to their own style: shorts, tops, sandals, jeans, t-shirts, tennis shoes, nail art, unconventional hair styles... you name it. But the thing that struck me the most, was what one of the senior leaders said as he welcomed them into the program. I cannot remember the exact words, but it was something along these lines: *"we don't know what the leader of the future will look like, what we do know is that it will be different from what we know today. We are not here to tell you who to become, or to mold you into a specific idea of a leader. We are here to give you the opportunity to experience different styles of leadership. What we want is for you to take from each what resonates and feels right, and combine them to create your very own style of leadership."*

At this point, I remember having goosebumps. What a wonderful example of Intergenerational Collaboration! Instead of expecting them to mold into the leader they had in mind, Unilever hired talent with huge potential, gave them the opportunity to work alongside many different leaders, and empowered them to decide what kind of leaders they wanted to become. Accepting that young talent is key to bringing the business into the future, and being open to putting their own leadership style on the table for young employees, not only to learn from but also to evaluate, is a great indicator of both vision and humility on the part of Unilever Baby Boomer and Gen X employees.

And while the young generations have the opportunity to learn from the experiences of older employees and their strong knowledge of the industry and the organization; the older generations can benefit from the ambition, drive and fresh perspective of the young ones, get a glimpse into what leadership will look like in the future, and use the information to map attributes to help them more accurately recruit talent with "future leadership" potential, helping the company stay ahead of the curve.

Empower Them and Make Them Feel Safe

We have heard it over and over again: Millennials and Gen Z want to **feel safe** at work. They know that making mistakes is part of the learning process, and that in order to become good at something they need to keep trying until they get it right. At the same time, they want to be able to contribute with their ideas and share their opinions openly and honestly. In short, they do not want to worry that the inevitable misstep will cost them their job or damage their career prospects. They want managers who **empower them** to take decisions, **protect them** if things go wrong, and **encourage them** to speak up, even when it means disagreeing with the status quo.

Ensuring that young talent feel at liberty to express their opinions is extremely important. An organization needs diverse viewpoints in order to experience renewal and innovation. When employees do not have the opportunity or the confidence to speak up, they lose motivation, become less engaged and eventually leave. Empowering people to fully participate and contribute is a leading business performance indicator. In markets or cultures where young people are taught not to question authority, however, this can be a challenge. In the traditional Asian culture, for example, speaking up, asking questions and sharing opinions has historically been discouraged. Children are instructed, from an early age, that it is best to remain silent because *"more talking, more mistakes; less talking, less mistakes"*. This fear of "showing off" or "losing face" translates into the workplace. Although things are changing — particularly as a result of the many multinational organizations that have set foot in the region and brought their open culture along with them — working alongside foreign employees, who are traditionally more outspoken, direct and vocal, can further inhibit and intimidate local employees.

While being a speaker at an event with Minna Rouru, Area HR Director Asia Pacific for **Kone**, I learned that the Finnish Engineering and Service Company experienced this problem firsthand. Despite its strong Nordic culture — open, collaborative and consensus-driven — Kone struggled to get full participation from young local employees, particularly in its Singapore office. Not only did their reluctance to openly participate stand in the way of their ambition and their desire to contribute, it also represented a significant business challenge; with no bench strength, the company found itself lacking local successors with the skills necessary to lead the business and its people.

In an effort to promote a culture of full participation, and to empower and enable local employees to speak their minds, Kone launched its **Emerging Leader Development Program** in Singapore. The program offered a strong combination of theory, practice and care. From developing communication-related competencies (learning how to deliver effective presentations, for example, gave people the confidence that they can — and know how to — influence decision-making) to giving cross-functional teams the opportunity to work on real-business challenges, emerging local leaders had the opportunity to put themselves forward, at their own pace, in an encouraging and supporting environment.

Minna shared with me that the prerequisite is a tone from the top that sets a culture where everyone is open to learn, and everyone is safe to voice their opinion. In Kone's case, what made a difference was the full commitment and support of senior leaders. *"In an MNC environment full of vocal and experienced expatriates, finding the confidence to speak up can be tough; but we need everyone's ideas and perspectives in order to move the business forward. After all, future success in the region is in the hands of the local talent. That's why we decided to put a lot of emphasis on the Management Team to create a culture of openness, care and encouragement that would empower our emerging local leaders to grow and shine. It soon became pretty clear that, regardless of their cultural backgrounds, when employees feel safe and supported, they develop the courage and confidence to contribute, share ideas, challenge and lead."*

The program changed the entire culture in Kone's Singapore team, and subsequently across the region. The company has reported higher engagement, involvement, drive and energy on the part of local employees. Building on the success of this initiative, Kone launched **Elevating Your Voice**, an event targeting female talent and encouraging them to perform, participate and voice their opinion.

Offer a Multi-Dimensional Path to Leadership

The reason why developing future leaders is such a challenge for most employers is that young talented people often prefer to leave an organization instead of having to figure out the politics and hidden barriers around moving up or across internally. The traditional "climb up the ladder" path to leadership is no longer in vogue. Unlike Gen X, who fresh out of school were already expected to "know" who they wanted to be five or ten years into the future (naturally, most Gen X did not have a clue, but there were countless books they were encouraged to read prior to job interviews that told them exactly how to answer that question), the new generations are open about the fact that they are human beings in the making. This means they may not yet know what they will be good at and what they will enjoy most. Hence, they cannot commit to a single career path. Instead, they seek employers who can help them learn and evolve with each new experience.

In 2019, I was scrolling rapidly down my LinkedIn feed, and my attention was suddenly captured by the picture of a beautiful plant sitting on a desk with a note: *"Watch Your Career GROW"*. It had been posted by someone working for **GroupM**, the world's largest media investment company. I found the idea of career advancement looking like a tree — with branches in all directions, of all shapes and sizes — extremely refreshing. After all, offering a path where employees do not have to follow one trajectory, but where new and exciting opportunities open up in front of them as they learn more about the world, the company and themselves, is exactly what the new generations crave. Hungry to find out more, I called Michael Wright, Global Head of Talent Acquisition at GroupM, whom I shared the stage with at leading industry conferences.

Michael told me that **GroupM Rotational Opportunities Workshop** (GROW) program was launched in April 2018 to address the young generation's desire to constantly evolve, learn, and explore new opportunities across different stages of their lives and careers. The goal was to retain talent and nurture diverse careers by designing paths to leadership that are not vertical or one-directional, but that bridge across networks and departments, and facilitating movement of employees into new roles with speed and fluidity without slowing down their careers. *"We don't believe in recruiting an employee just once. We believe in curated careers — and this means recruiting talent CONTINUALLY. With GROW's skills mapping and development plans, we identify transferable skills that people can take from job to job and client to client, and we are able to carefully curate pathways across clients, practices, countries, and find a new home for our employees to flourish. This not only benefits our business by allowing us to tap into our own people's unique skillsets, but it forms a culture of transparency, trust and support. When your people are happy — continuously learning and given the opportunity to grow over time — your business is happy and so are your clients,"* Michael said.

GroupM is not the first employer to launch internal mobility programs, but what is unique about GROW is that it aims to promote x-company mobility within the group. This speaks volumes of its commitment towards developing talent and making sure employees find the path that works best for them. *"GroupM is a collective. A Company of Companies! Each GroupM Company has its own distinct culture, its own global, regional and local leadership teams, and its own unique programs and specialties. While our main businesses compete with agency, technology, consulting and media companies for clients and talent, at the same time, growing an employee's career across agency has not been traditionally part of our culture. People used to grow vertically. What makes me so proud of GROW is that it connects us as a group and we can now offer horizontal paths,"* Michael added.

The other aspect I like about GROW is that it addresses young talent's concern that pursuing different career options within the same organization may hurt their career or their relationship with their manager. When employees want to explore new opportunities, they raise their hand in confidentiality. The GROW team led by Gillian Ramos — a young Millennial leader — works with them to identify the role that best suits them and supports them in developing the required skills. The employees' managers are only notified once an appropriate match is made. In the first two years of GROW, 175 employees graduated from the program. To celebrate their achievement, once they successfully transferred to their new internal role, they received as congratulatory items a GROW mug that resembles a planter, and a "growing" pencil (yes, a pencil that they can plant after use!).

Give Them Exposure and Allow Them to Make an Impact — From Shadow Boards to Leadership and Impact Challenges

The new generations crave visibility and access to leadership. At the same time, organizations — as we saw earlier in the case of **Procter & Gamble** — need the New Age mindset and the understanding of young consumers that only late Millennials and early Gen Z can bring to the table. From **Gucci** to **AccorHotels**, more organizations are inserting young employees into their Boards in an effort to cover "blind spots" in decision-making and inject fresh perspective into the Company.

During my conversation with Michael, I also learned that GroupM is one of the first organizations to create what is now known as a "**Shadow Board**", a group of young employees with leadership potential who work alongside the Executive Committee on strategic initiatives.

Rohit Suri, Chief HR & Talent Officer, **GroupM India**, shared with me that the YCO, or **Youth Committee Program**, was launched in India in 2013 not only to address the company's need for a cultural and digital transformation, but also to meet young talent's growing demand for shorter and more impactful paths to leadership. *"Hiring the very best talent requires a strong commitment. The young generations have a lot of energy, they are aspirational, and have high learning and absorption needs. Not only do they want to do things that are meaningful, but they also want to make an impact quickly. You must be able to offer them the opportunity to connect with the right people within the organization. When young talent can learn directly from senior leaders, they are more likely to stay and grow with the business; at the same time, senior leaders benefit from their fresh inputs, which they can obtain quickly without hierarchies or bottlenecks. It's a win-win situation,"* Rohit said.

The GroupM YCO members are 15 of the top performers with highest potential for leadership, under 30 years of age, and who have been with the company for more than one year. YCOs become the sounding board of the Executive Committee (ExCo) and work on projects of organizational importance that go beyond their regular day job. *"The Executive Committee is the senior-most level of the organization; the Youth Committee members are at the bottom of the pyramid. Technology has brought a lot of disruption to our industry and we need to know the new trends. Young generations are much more in tune with these new trends than the older ones who are running the organization, so there is a significant gap. The YCO program aims to close this gap through* **Constant Feedback**, **Strategic Projects** *and* **Reverse Mentoring**,*"* Rohit said.

1. **Constant Feedback**. When the Executive Committee identifies a new area of focus — or when there are business critical projects — the YCOs are brought in for a round of feedback. The goal is to hear what

the organization as a whole is thinking, whether the plans that are being made at the top make sense, and to leverage the YCOs perspective to shape the strategy. This is particularly valuable when the company is looking at a product or service targeted towards younger audiences, as the younger generations can contribute in a more meaningful way.

2. **Strategic Projects**. During the course of the year, the ExCo members identify one or two strategic projects that the YCO members will take charge of and present back to the ExCo. Two examples are: a series of initiatives related to **Organizational Wellness**, and a program to address the critical need to **Upskill** employees. To help employees reorientate themselves to the new products that are available in the market, the Youth Committee launched **GroupM Champions League** (GCL), a gamified learning experience offering 30 different learning programs. The YCO came up with the idea, developed the technology, drafted the entire communication and launched it. In the first three months of GCL, the company gave out 15,000 certifications. I will talk more about the GroupM Champions League in Chapter 27 on **Life-long Learning**.

3. **Reverse Mentoring**. During the course of the year, each ExCo member is mentored by two YCOs on two different areas. These are identified based on the interest of the ExCo and the expertise of the YCO. It could be about **New Technologies** — such as *Machine Learning*, *Block Chain*, *eSport*, *Social Media Trends*, *New Age Gaming* or *Programmatic*; **Business** — such as *Brand Advocacy in the Digital Age*, *Storytelling for Selling and Pitching*, *Team Cultures Effect on Productivity*, *Gross Happiness Index Implementation in the Corporate World*, or *Influencer Strategies*; or **Wellness** — such as *The Importance of Being Fit*, *Work–Life Balance*, *How Passions Beyond Work Can Benefit One's Career*, even *The Future of Football in India*. During scheduled sessions, the YCOs walk the ExCo through their understanding of the topic. This leads to healthy debates that provide a great learning opportunity for both generations. I will cover more about this in Chapter 26 on **Reverse-Mentoring**.

Shadow Boards are one of the best examples of both Intergenerational Collaboration and the positive impact it has on the business. Some of the youngest and most talented members of the organization work alongside the most senior and experienced industry leaders — not as subordinates, but as advisors — making valuable contributions and together shaping the future of the organization. The downside is that, because of its nature, this type of exposure can only be offered to a small number of employees. Having a Shadow Board also requires a progressive mindset and a strong level of commitment that many organizations may not yet be ready for.

There are, however, other ways to give ambitious young talent the opportunity to work on high-impact projects and gain exposure to leadership. One way is through **Company Business Challenges**. I will share a few examples of very well-known and successful ones.

Unilever Future Leaders' League Hackathon. Here, bright young minds from all over the world have the opportunity to make an impact by submitting their ideas on how technology can accelerate Unilever's goal to make sustainable living commonplace. The top teams are shortlisted to compete at the yearly *International London Grand Finals*, presenting their idea to top global senior leaders in front of top students from around the world. The winners have the opportunity to gig-work with the brand team and join the Unilever delegation at the **One Young World Summit**.

L'Oréal Brandstorm innovation competition. Here, selected students from 60 countries are given the chance to tackle a real business case and innovate some of L'Oréal's 24 international brands, under the guidance of academic mentors and L'Oréal employee coaches.

P&G CEO Challenge. Here, young talent with exceptional aptitude for business strategy and real-life problem-solving compete with peers from around the world to see who is most fit to be the next CEO of P&G. Top students win an all-expense paid trip to the location of the Regional Finals where they have the opportunity to network with P&G leaders, compete for a place at the *Global Final*, and win the opportunity to meet with the Global CEO of P&G and other CEOs from top companies.

Cisco Global Problem Solver Challenge. Here, student entrepreneurs from around the world present new business ideas that leverage technology for social impact. Winners receive USD350,000 in prize money to help accelerate the adoption of breakthrough technology, products, and services that drive economic development and/or solve social or environmental problems.

Hackathons and other leadership challenges aside, **Entrepreneurship** and **Intrapreneurship Programs** that help young ambitious youth take their big idea and turn into a real scalable initiative for their employer are rapidly gaining momentum. One such example is **The Nudge Academy**, an eight-month online personal development program where 90 young professionals from around the world come together to learn about leadership, sustainability and impact creation. During the program they come up with an impact plan and apply for the **Nudge Global Impact Award** where they have the opportunity to pitch the result of their plan to an international jury and VIPs in the world-famous *Peace Palace in The Hague*.

The **Nudge Global Impact Challenge** was designed to help companies develop sustainable leadership skills for their young high-potential employees, and fulfill their need to make a difference by giving them an opportunity to turn their high-impact idea into reality. The young professionals who participate in the Nudge Academy are required to be curious, look inside their organization and come up with ideas and projects that would not only benefit their employers' bottom line, but also contribute to one or more of the Sustainable Development Goals. Throughout the program, they learn how to turn this idea into a business plan, how to align it with the overall strategy of the company, how to create momentum in the organization to execute on the plan, and finally they get to execute it.

A young **Heineken** employee in Vietnam was able to build a bridge from the recycled crown corks of Tiger beer bottles. This bridge crosses a canal connecting two communities in Tien Giang: Năng Canal, Tam Hiệp Ward, Châu Thành District, Tiền Giang Province An Giang: Hòa Bình Canal, Phú

Thành Ward, Phú Tân District, An Giang Province. Before the bridge was built, inhabitants of the two communities had to walk miles and miles down the canal before reaching a crossing that would allow them to connect and trade.

Aside from Heineken, organizations that have signed up their top young talent for the program include **ABN Amro**, **Capgemini**, **The China Navigation Co**, **Swire Shipping**, **BMW Group**, **Ferrero** and **Siemens**. *"These organizations are much aware that this new generation of employees is not only interested in a well-paying job with growth opportunities, but heavily prioritizes employers that have a purpose and are committed to finding solutions to big issues, such as climate change, erosion of ecosystems, gender equality, poverty reduction and so forth. Leaders are realizing that innovation grows from 'within', and that in an environment that is changing at light speed, they need to leverage the fresh perspectives, innovative ideas, technical skills and wide networks of their future leaders,"* Jan van Betten, Founder of Nudge Global Impact Challenge, shared with me.

Another way organizations are showing their commitment towards developing both young leaders and their ideas, is giving employees the opportunity to allocate part of their working hours towards a passion project of their choice. Although **Google's 20% Time** initiative allowing employees to dedicate 20 percent of their working time to a side project is what put this type of initiative on the radar in 2004 (it even resulted in *Adsense* and *Google News*), 3M has had a similar policy in place since 1948. The **3M 15% Culture** was meant to encourage employees to *"set aside a portion of their work time to proactively cultivate and pursue innovative ideas that excite them."*

Unilever is another organization that has used this concept to democratize career experiences and learning by matching employees to passion-projects based on areas of interest and skillsets. Whenever the company identifies a match, employees receive an email. If they are interested in taking up the project, they speak to their line manager, after which they can start to dedicate 10-20 percent of their time to it.

According to **Bosch** — another employer with a strong focus on motivating creative thinking and innovative problem solving by giving employees time and space to work on projects that go beyond their regular job — *"enabling intrapreneurship can allow organizations to introduce an innovative mindset. Introducing cross-division brainstorm sessions, working with tech start-ups, organizing hackathons and providing mentorship and funding for internal projects are some steps that companies can take to promote an intrapreneur spirit within organizations."*

Chapter 26

Encourage a Learning Exchange: Two-Way Mentoring, Reverse Mentoring and Other Initiatives

"Leadership and Learning Are Indispensable to Each Other."

— *John F. Kennedy*

In a multigenerational environment, it is important to ensure that everyone's strengths and contributions are acknowledged. As the workplace has evolved alongside technological advances, employees of different age groups might feel that there is little appreciation for what they bring to the table, simply because they are all contributing in different ways and have built their expertise on different platforms. *"New Age skills are different from the ones that Baby Boomers have been exposed to throughout most of their careers; this can make them feel left out, or that the organization gives too much importance to younger talent's abilities and too little to their many years of experience. At the same time, young generations are impatient to demonstrate their skills and make an impact, and often view some of their older managers as blockers. There is clearly always a tussle, and while this can be healthy, it's important to ensure employees understand and are willing to leverage what other generations can bring to the table,"* Pallavi Srivastava, Talent Leader, Global Technology Services Asia Pacific (APAC) and Greater China for **IBM**, said to me during one of our periodic coffee catch-ups.

One of the most effective strategies to build mutual respect and ensure that young and senior employees value and benefit from each other's strengths, is giving them the opportunity to learn from one another through

Cross-Generational Mentoring Programs. Instead of traditional Mentoring, where senior employees coach the young ones, **Two-Way Mentoring** and **Reverse Mentoring** are a much more effective way to help promote knowledge transfer and Intergenerational Collaboration.

In the *XYZ@Work 2020 Multigenerational Workforce Study*, 89 percent of Gen Z students said that having Reverse Mentoring or similar initiatives to promote better collaboration and sharing between generations would make an employer significantly more attractive to them.

In **Reverse Mentoring** young employees advise senior leaders. We have seen this with **GroupM India**, where members of the Youth Committee advise members of the Executive Committee.

Unilever is another organization with a strong focus on Reverse Mentoring. The company has recently developed an Artificial Intelligence platform with Gloat — called **Flex Experiences** — where senior employees (mentees) are matched with young employees (mentors) who coach them on topics that include new trends in technology, young consumer preferences and new ways of thinking.

Two-Way Mentoring is the perfect way to leverage both the experience of Baby Boomers and Gen X, and the digital expertise of Millennials and Gen Z. In **Two-Way Mentoring**, young and senior employees are both mentor and mentee, taking turns learning from one another based on their own areas of expertise. The senior employee, for example, could coach the young one on working with clients, while at the same time being advised on how to minimize data integrity issues.

Although, to my surprise, few organizations have Cross-Generational Mentoring Programs, the concept itself is nothing new. Reverse Mentoring was first introduced by Jack Welch, Global CEO of **General Electric** from 1981 to 2001. In 1999, in an effort to get his Leadership Team to learn how to use the web, he paired 500 executives with young employees who showed them their way around the internet.

When it comes to the need for senior employees to brush up on their digital skills, nothing could have exacerbated it more than the Covid-19 Pandemic. With most countries around the world on some sort of lockdown and people working from home, employees of all ages have had to rely exclusively on digital tools to perform their duties. I have a number of Millennial friends who told me about the countless phone calls they received from their Baby Boomer or early Gen X bosses and colleagues during lockdown asking them for support with their tech tools while working from home. The ability to use software tools such as Zoom, Confluence, JIRA, Microsoft Teams, Mural, and Slack — for time management, project management, meetings, presentations, team communications, design, development and file sharing — has quickly become essential. This has been a wake-up call for many older employees who have been relying on traditional ways of conducting business.

Procter & Gamble is one of the few organizations that has addressed the need for senior leaders to get up-to-speed with the new technologies well ahead of Covid-19. In 2017, the company launched a formal program in China where every member of the Leadership Team is paired with a Reverse Coach — a young Millennial from the IT department who can teach them everything from coding, block-chain and new apps available in the market, to how the internet works or what goes behind a web address. *"The program was born out of the recognition that digitizing the workforce is a critical strategy and that strengthening the Digital Quotient (DQ) of our entire organization is what will enable us to sustain our competitive advantage,"* Rene Co explained to me. *"Many of us in the Leadership Team or in Senior Management didn't grow up in a digital world, and while the young generations are digital natives, we are digital immigrants. We need to ensure that our senior leaders are equipped to use the new technology that is continuously being rolled out, and that we are trained to think about digital solutions to make our daily work better."* The program has received strong support by P&G leadership including Mathew Price, President of P&G Greater China, who personally role-models it.

With the Covid-19 Pandemic disrupting the workforce and restricting face-to-face interaction between employees, organizations had to adapt. In 2020, in response to the lock-down, **Citi** launched **Two-Way Crowd Reverse Mentoring** as part of their focus on driving generational inclusion through organizational empathy. Unlike the standard Reverse Mentoring approach involving one mentor and one mentee, the one-hour exchange takes place once a month for four consecutive months over Zoom between nine people: a Coach from the *Generations Affinity* working committee, four employees who are either Traditionalists, Baby Boomers or Gen X, and four who are either Millennials or Gen Z. Participants — who do not know each other prior to the session — range from Analysts to Managing Directors from different functions or businesses. In order to ensure maximum engagement and relevance, the Coach presents a set of topics for the participants to vote on, designs a series of questions, sends them to everyone in advance and moderates the discussion. Topics range from e-sports, "banking versus start-ups" in the competition for talent, "turning coffee into your next job or client" and "the latest and greatest social media platforms and how to use them".

Citi is a great example of how organizations can get creative with their Cross-Generational Mentoring Programs. They can also be a great platform to discuss diversity-related issues in a non-threatening way. For example, aside from teaching digital skills, **Procter & Gamble** has also used Reverse Mentoring to pair young female employees (mentors) to senior male managers (mentees). This initiative gave young talented women the opportunity to become more visible within the organization, and naturally resulted in increased retention rates of female employees.

Regardless of their objective — or whether Reverse and Two-Way Mentoring programs have a structured format or one that is left up to the mentors and their mentees to agree upon — both require a strong commitment from both the young and the old generations. A lot of thought also needs to be given to finding the right match between mentor and mentee. Not only should they be paired based on their experience, skillsets, or expertise but also, and most importantly, based on **cultural and personality fit**. Highlighting similarities between different individuals, regardless of age, is a great way to help people find common ground and ensure they bond with each other, creating an environment of trust and belonging.

Surprisingly, in the *XYZ@Work 2020 Multigenerational Workforce Study* of more than 250 HR Professionals, only 16 percent said their company has a formal Reverse or Two-Way Mentoring program. Those that do, ask the younger generations to mentor Baby Boomers and Gen X predominantly on: social media, technology, digital media, mobile apps, creativity and innovation, flexibility, agility and new ways of thinking. The older generations, on the other hand, mentor Millennials and Gen Z on: how to sell to clients or build an internal network, storytelling, leadership, communication skills, executive presence, strategic thinking, risk management, conflict resolution and work ethics.

Aside from work-related skills, there are other initiatives that promote cross-generational learning. These include **Buddy Pairings**, where junior and senior employees take turns to teach each other something that is non-work related, such as cooking, how to live a zero-waste life, how to use a video software or how to build a fanbase on social media.

For those companies that are not able to commit to a formal program, similar outcomes can be achieved through **Collective Sharing**. **Internal Ted X** events are a great way to ensure employees from all age groups can benefit and learn from the wealth of knowledge that surrounds them. With Covid-19, we have also seen the rise of virtual sessions where Baby Boomer and Gen X leaders share their knowledge with the younger generation as a way to give back, engage the youth and stay relevant. Millennials and Gen Z also share insights about how they think, feel and make decisions as both employees and consumers.

Finally, on a day-to-day basis, feedback, feedback and more feedback is critical. Structured or unstructured, as long as it is mutual and frequent, and as long as employers can create an atmosphere where people from different generations can openly and constructively share and learn from each other without fear.

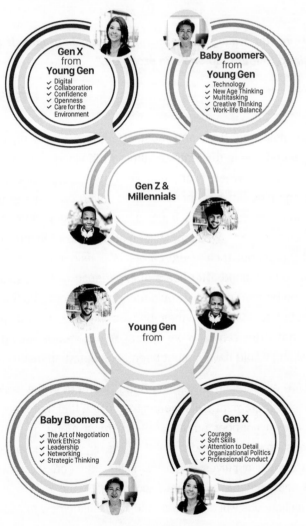

SKILLS GENERATIONS WANT TO
LEARN FROM EACH OTHER

Gen X from **Young Gen**
- Digital
- Collaboration
- Confidence
- Openness
- Care for the Environment

Baby Boomers from **Young Gen**
- Technology
- New Age Thinking
- Multitasking
- Creative Thinking
- Work-life Balance

Gen Z & Millennials

Young Gen from

Baby Boomers
- The Art of Negotiation
- Work Ethics
- Leadership
- Networking
- Strategic Thinking

Gen X
- Courage
- Soft Skills
- Attention to Detail
- Organizational Politics
- Professional Conduct

Figure 52

Chapter 27

Advocate and Practice Life-long Learning

"If you are not willing to learn, no one can help you. If you are determined to learn, no one can stop you."

— *Zig Ziglar*

One of the most important and most effective ways to bridge the gap between generations is to create a culture of life-long learning across the entire organization. When everybody is continuously being upskilled or reskilled, regardless of age, nobody feels called out. This is particularly important when we take into account the different generational attitudes towards "being trained". While for Millennials and Gen Z being continuously developed throughout their entire career is considered a non-negotiable, the idea of being trained after years of experience was not something the average Baby Boomer or Gen X would feel thrilled about. Older generations were expected to learn from their bosses when they first entered the workforce, but after ten or more years of experience, being told they needed training would have almost been considered an insult.

Increased life expectancy is keeping Baby Boomers in the workforce well past the age of retirement. This means they often find themselves in direct competition with younger employees who have many of the skills that organizations now deem fundamental. However, with the speed at which AI is transforming our lives, even the skills that young people possess today will soon not be sufficient. According to the *Future Jobs Report 2018*, 75 million jobs will disappear, and 133 million new roles will emerge by 2022, all of which require either strong technical knowledge or the ability to work alongside AI to improve productivity and efficiencies. These numbers will accelerate as a result of the Covid-19 Pandemic, and success will more than ever depend on employees' ability to transform by moving frequently between tasks, cultures and business models. **Siemens**, for example, started training a large number of non-engineers to do jobs engineers would have done in the past, in an effort to fill its increasing roles requiring technical knowledge.

With the rapid rate of change we are experiencing; nobody is truly prepared for *The Future of Work*. On one hand, most educational institutions fail to teach students the necessary skills that will make them easily employable; on the other, older generations have not been encouraged to acquire the new skills required to stay relevant in the workforce. Whether you are a Baby Boomer, a Gen X, a Millennial or a Gen Z, not being an agile, life-long learner in this new environment is simply not an option.

The concept of life-long learning gained a lot of momentum after **Microsoft** rolled out its **Growth Mindset Management Framework**. Growth Mindset is founded on the premise that when employees become eager to learn, their skills improve and they achieve more over time. In short, if people believe in their own ability to develop, and are given the opportunity to continuously expand their thinking by learning new things, they will continue to evolve. This is where upskilling and reskilling programs come into play. According to *PwC 2019 Global CEO Survey*, organizations that have advanced programs cited stronger corporate culture and employee engagement, greater innovation and accelerated digital transformation, increased ability to attract and retain talent, and higher workforce productivity. However, only 18 percent of organizations globally made significant progress in establishing an upskilling program.

Nonetheless, **Microsoft** and **Siemens** are not alone. **Unilever**, **DBS** and **GroupM** have also shown a strong commitment towards ensuring that all their employees, regardless of age, remain relevant and employable.

Unilever has developed **The Future of Work Framework**, where all employees are supported to develop a **Future Fit Development Plan** where the focus is: identifying their purpose and the role it plays in the work they do; coming up with plans to ensure their own wellbeing; and mapping their current skills gap to ascertain what competencies they need to develop or work on. This exercise helps employees determine their future career options, such as whether they want to upskill — by further developing their existing skills but keeping them in their current job — or reskill — by learning similar or different skillsets than the ones they currently possess to prepare them for new jobs.

Similarly, **DBS'** approach to managing a Multigenerational Workforce recognizes the diverse career and life experiences of its employees. The financial services group is an exceptional case study, as its entire philosophy of upskilling and reskilling is centered on tailoring programs to individual professional growth, building emotional confidence, and forming communities. Strengthening **the emotional connection** with employees across generational cohorts is fundamental in order to build a collaborative learning culture. Even more so for organizations that will need to redeploy a large number of employees to new roles within the company.

During our conversation, Ng Ying Yuan, Chief Operating Officer for Group Human Resources at DBS, said something that strongly resonates with me. *"It's human nature: when we do something and we are good at it, it becomes part of our identity and we grow attached to it. This is the case for many of our employees. We want to encourage them to revisit their own narratives, realize that even though they love their job, there are new interesting roles coming up for them to grow into, and that their identity as a professional can continue to change and evolve. This is why addressing the emotive angle is so important."*

But encouraging employees to embrace change is not enough. Older generations are often worried that they may not be able to learn quickly enough, or pick up new digital skills as easily as the younger generations. If an organization does not provide the right learning environment, any effort to upskill or reskill them will prove ineffective. To address this, DBS has set out to galvanize employees by building shared purpose across the bank, which in turn enables the design of common rituals and ways of working and learning together.

"Revisiting their own professional identities can make senior employees feel vulnerable. Learning new skills alongside someone who is younger and faster can be intimidating. This made us think long and hard about designing learning experiences where employees with diverse career histories and learning needs can muster the confidence and the right mindset to embrace learning," Ng Ying Yuan said.

In 2017, DBS launched a program to build confidence in learning among senior employees. The idea was to get them together in an auditorium along with their friends for a day of fun and games, free food, and a lucky draw. DBS ran the event using **Appreciative Inquiry**, a behavioral science approach to running large skill interventions. Appreciative Inquiry uses people's past positive memories as a motivator to take on other new similar experiences.

"We asked our employees to think about a time when they picked up a new hobby or tried something completely new, and it turned into a positive experience. By talking about it, we were able to ride on that positive energy and help them realize that it could be just as easy, fun and enjoyable for them to pick up a new simple skill, like using an iPad to serve customers or taking a LinkedIn Learning class on human-centered design. Getting them to share their experiences with their friends provided the peer support and encouragement for them to be open to upskilling and reskilling, without feeling vulnerable or threatened," Ng Ying Yuan went on sharing.

In the post-Covid-19 world, DBS' focus on lifelong learning now comes with a greater sense of urgency. As the company reimagines its future for business, customers and society, DBS continues to emphasize not just the skills and tools needed by its employees, but also embracing a growth mindset in this New Normal.

According to Rohit Suri, Chief HR Officer, **GroupM** India, another great way to create a culture where learning new skills becomes an exciting, non-threatening experience, is to create a **pull factor**. In August 2019, the company launched **GroupM Champions League**, a three-month gamified and highly curated upskilling program with a prize at the end. The company created unique learning journeys for each set of employees based on the skills that would benefit them the most, and offered more than 100 classroom, webinar and mixed modules training courses for digital upskilling. Each employee was assigned a number of training modules to complete, classified by level of difficulty. Participants were split into teams, and every time an employee completed a module, the team would gain points. The number of points was directly related to the level of difficulty of the program, how many people completed their program, and how quickly. The points were updated live in a dashboard that the entire organization could access. *"We created a pull factor by leveraging our employees' competitive spirit. The push then came from people within each team calling upon each other to complete tasks so that the team could win. But the best part was that employees started supporting each other. If someone struggled with a particular module, other team members would offer to help, This created a support ecosystem where everyone was able to deliver. GCL worked beautifully: learning became not only a game, but also a collaborative experience,"* Rohit said.

In the three-months of GCL alone, GroupM handed out more than 15,000 certifications. The program strengthened the learning culture of the organization and created great momentum for employees to take part in the many other upskilling programs offered by the company throughout the year. All in all, in 2019, with a headcount of approximately 2,500 employees, GroupM India delivered 92 training courses to 1,611 participants in a classroom setting and 47 programs to 3,556 participants digitally. In addition, during Covid-19, the company opened up a series of new programs to make sure employees continued their learning journey, and prepared for the late 2020 launch of GCL 2.0.

Finally, a culture of life-long learning has the added benefit of decreasing attrition rates among younger employees. Aside from intergenerational conflicts, the other reason why the youngest members of the workforce leave an organization is that they feel they **stopped learning**.

Whether this is true or not, learning does tend to slow down after the first couple of years. To a certain extent, this is due to a failure on the part of employers to set the right expectations. Let's think about it for a moment. Many organizations hire students fresh out of school and put them through incredible programs with a steep learning curve. After the program ends and the "real job" begins, things naturally wind down. If the organization does not make a conscious effort to ensure their young employees feel they are constantly developing, they risk investing precious time and resources training individuals who will take those learnings elsewhere.

Chapter 28

Intergenerational Collaboration: the Key to Family Business Succession

While conflicts between generations are detrimental in any organization, they can have devastating consequences in family-owned businesses. Interpersonal dynamics between relatives are even more complicated than they are between strangers, particularly in more traditional cultures, where children are expected to listen to their elders and follow the chain of command.

During the many sessions I have run with family-owned businesses, Next-Gens have consistently expressed frustration stemming from their desire to be more involved in key decision-making and to be allowed to align the company mission to causes they feel passionate about. First-generation owners (G1s), on the other hand, have openly admitted to being concerned about Next-Gens' ability to lead the business into the future. Their biggest concerns are related to incompetence, laziness, failure to ensure continuity, lack of trust, and a sense of entitlement. Furthermore, the high expectations and controlling nature of G1s — who having founded the company often believe they know best — are a big burden on Next-Gens, who have the responsibility to carry forward the family legacy, appeal to an entire new generation of consumers, and face unprecedented challenges due to a rapidly evolving landscape, all while making sure that they do not jeopardize what was built before them.

As a result, unable to assert themselves and establish credibility with older family members, an increasing number of Next-Gens are leaving the family business. *"Those of us who are predestined to take over our parents' company are often expected to transition seamlessly into the organization.*

We feel a tremendous amount of pressure to earn the respect of employees, managers, customers, consultants, partners and family board members alike. At the same time, we don't have the freedom to move the company in the direction that we believe is best or link it to what we are passionate about, because the previous generation is unwilling to relinquish or even share control," a 26-year-old Next-Gen told me during a workshop in 2018.

William, the heir of a **Real Estate Investment Company** whom I spoke to in the early part of 2020, shared with me that the process of taking over the family business has been over-complicated predominantly by the difference in mindset between himself, a Gen X, and his father, a Traditionalist. *"Most of the issues stemmed largely from his 'I know what I am doing' mentality and his reluctance to trust what he cannot understand. His past success engendered his belief that he will be able to navigate today's challenges with the same tools and the same thinking. He does not understand that things have changed. For example, he believes marketing is the same now as it was 30 years ago and hence our General Manager should be on top of it."*

When a business faces opposing agendas, lack of collaboration between family members, or conflicts between siblings, it is unlikely to carry on across generations. In fact, Aik-Ping Ng, Co-Head, Family Office Advisory, Asia Pacific and Senior Family Governance Advisor at **HSBC Private Banking** in Hong Kong, shared with me that fewer than one-third of family businesses survive from the first to the second generation; and even fewer are able to pass on their companies to the third generation. Many rise quickly, attaining impressive success, but do not survive a generational change in leadership. Fortune Magazine reported that in the 1960s, the average lifespan of a company in the Standard & Poor's (S&P) index was roughly 60 years, whereas today it is closer to 20 years.

As Niall Glynn wrote in *Planning for Family Business Succession*, *"too often, family businesses replicate the skills and practices of the past without examining wider changes in the external marketplace"*. In a VUCA world, organizations who cannot innovate are unlikely to survive, and businesses require both operational excellence and deep experience across many different areas in order to prosper. When Next-Gen is either unwilling or incapable of taking the business forward, the course of action often becomes to professionalize the business and secure an exit via a sale or listing.

According to Aik-Ping, *"in order to ensure family business succession or continuity, harmonizing a Multigenerational Workforce is central to properly harnessing the qualitative capital existing within the family. During the stewardship and legacy phases of the wealth cycle, a long-term perspective is needed to ensure that all family members are working to uphold their business' reputation and stability."*

This is particularly important as we face the effects of the Covid-19 Pandemic. While periods of upheavals can raise concerns and uncertainties in multigenerational family businesses, they are also a good time to have discussions about the future — not just about financial wealth, but considerations such as the legacy one leaves behind.

Unleashing the power of Intergenerational Collaboration requires, on both sides, humility and openness to learn. G1s must understand that upcoming leadership will face strong challenges that will require **agility**, **adaptability** and **innovation**. To ensure the business can withstand these challenges, they must be aware that past management skills and styles may no longer be effective. They need to prepare the Next-Gen for leadership by involving them early on, and allowing them to shape the direction of the business through their knowledge of young consumers and the environment around them. *"The older generations can impart a lot of knowledge onto the younger ones, including a set of timeless principles such as being true to one's word, the importance of cultivating relationships, how to earn respect of employees and customers, how to focus and avoid distraction. However, the application of these principles in business may not be the same today, hence it's important for G1s to give the younger generation the opportunity to think through and decide how to apply them in today's rapidly changing world."* At the same time, they need to make an effort to listen more patiently and understand the perspectives and rationale of the younger generation without being dismissive. *"This is difficult for older generations, because if they attempt to understand something, they may find themselves unable to do so, which naturally they don't want to be forced to admit,"* William said to me.

Next-Gens, on the other hand, need to make an effort to understand the psychology, habits, patterns and triggers of the older generations, and use **empathy**, **sensibility** and **tact** when trying to get their point across. Learning how they prefer to communicate and interact can go a long way towards improving collaboration and creating trust. For example, when questioning the rationale of G1s, instead of saying *"tell me your rationale and let's see **if it makes sense**"*, choose *"walk me through your rationale **so I can learn from you**"*. Removing egotism from the process allows family members to address issues for impact, rather than turning them into a case of who is right and who is wrong.

Family-owned businesses are perfect to showcase the power of Intergenerational Collaboration: all they can accomplish with it, and all they can lose without it. Those that manage to steer away from toxic family dynamics and focus instead on leveraging unique perspectives, are able to fully harness the power of each generation by combining the extensive experience of the current leaders with the innovative mindset of the future ones. When there are two or three passionate generations involved, what is often seen as a recipe for disaster, can quickly become a company's biggest competitive advantage. Furthermore, solidified relationships in family businesses can promote cohesion and pride in a company that prospers from one generation to the next. This motivates family members and staff to elevate their standards and work harder to ensure the business continues to thrive.

While writing this book, I had a series of conversations with **HSBC Private Banking**. I wanted to understand, from their long-standing history of serving family businesses and facilitating dialogues between different family stakeholders, what they have found to be the most important steps a family-owned business should take in order to preserve family legacy and ensure smooth transition between generations. You can see the nine steps for **Empowering Business Families to Survive and Thrive for the Next Lap** in Figure 53.

FOOD FOR THOUGHT:
EMPOWERING BUSINESS FAMILIES TO SURVIVE AND THRIVE FOR THE NEXT LAP

- Encouraging open communication: Every member of the family must make an honest effort to understand each other's perspective, fears and concerns.

- Building trust catalysts across teams: Create projects to bring together otherwise siloed functional teams and to build mutual trust.

- Improving communication processes and tools: Formalize communication channels and review existing norms of communication to determine what has or has not worked in the past.

- Establishing and strengthening connections: Take a break to bond as a team outside of the family environment and the office.

- Embarking on family projects and endeavors: When family members collaborate on projects together, it builds solidarity around a common mission and purpose.

- Leading by example: the leaders of a family business can shape the culture from the top down.

- Creating family constitutions and testimonials: crystallize the legacies, traditions and heritage that epitomizes the family history.

- Clarifying priorities, roles and responsibilities: Identify potential sources of tension to develop effective decision-making mechanisms.

- Establishing a family or business trust for intergenerational wealth transfer and using private trust companies ("PTC") to help some ultra-high-net-worth families retain control and ownership of their family businesses.

Figure 53

To this I would only add: allow them to link the company to a new or bigger purpose, especially one they are passionate about. With Gen Z in particular, this will be paramount.

Chapter 29

Now It's Up To You!

Throughout this book I have taken you on a journey through time. We started by looking at the events that made Generational Diversity an important business imperative, including the Millennial Workplace Revolution, the rise of Gen Z, the impact of the Covid-19 Pandemic, and *The Future of Work*. We then focused on the history and evolution of peer groups to analyze the key attributes that set generations apart, and how empathy and understanding can turn generational differences into a competitive advantage. Finally, we had a backstage view on how leading global organizations strongly committed to Generational Diversity have addressed generational differences, the types of programs and initiatives they deployed, and the approaches they have taken.

With the rapid rate of change our society is undergoing, organizations need to continuously adapt, which means developing leaders who are able to cope in times of crisis and deep uncertainty. Alongside technology, **Diversity and Inclusion** will play a major part in this transformation journey, as without it, creativity and innovation will suffer and solutions cannot be sustained.

While generational differences are often overlooked, buried under the sand, or simply ignored, they will now play major part in either stagnating progress or catalyzing change. Our world is in desperate need of both the experience and knowledge of the older generations, and the energy and social mindedness of today's youth. While Millennials and Gen Z understand what is important to society at large, they need the support of Baby Boomers and Gen X to turn their aspirations into practice.

To harness the power of every generation, the working environment is paramount. Organizations must ensure that the difference in mindsets between the young and the old generations do not hinder performance and innovation. To do this, they must commit to fostering a culture where everyone feels equally valuable, respected, recognized, and able to contribute. The disparities and hidden resentments, however, can make this unachievable. The only way to overcome this barrier is to embrace generational differences and — without diminishing the importance of individuality — accept that stereotypes exist because people adhere to commonalities, and understanding the context that shaped us and those around us is the key to finding ways to work better with one other.

Business leaders play a big part in helping employees reframe the generational stereotype, foster collaboration, embrace diversity and drive positive change. A good starting point is to level the playing field through a deeper understanding of the hopes and fears of each generation. Baby Boomers and Gen X worry about being seen as obsolete, considered out-of-place in environments that are increasingly digital and agile. Millennials and Gen Z, on the other hand, worry about not being heard or able to drive change. Until these fears are put to rest, it will be virtually impossible for senior employees to pass down their knowledge and experience to the new generations effectively, prepare them for leadership and empower them to drive impact and innovation.

Leading organizations around the world are increasingly committed to making Generational Diversity a key item on their Diversity and Inclusion agendas. Establishing a series of initiatives to encourage intergenerational awareness and bonding, using collaborative decision-making to create winning multigenerational teams, helping leaders shift into a New-Age mindset, holding managers accountable for their employees' success, preparing young generations for leadership through impact and empowerment, and establishing a culture of cross-generational and life-long learning have proven to be winning strategies in helping to bridge the generational divide and harness the strengths of each generation.

But at the end of the day, it is up to each and every one of us. We all have a responsibility to create a nurturing and inclusive work environment. For this, we need curiosity and a genuine desire to learn from others, but also a deep understanding of ourselves, our own biases, and how our values and behaviors affect those around us. Basic communication — even among peers — is complicated enough. When you add generational dynamics, you have one more layer of complexity that often becomes a barrier for positive collaboration. We can address this by being authentic and leveraging our own personal strengths, but flexing when necessary to ensure that we are able to set others up for success.

I strongly believe that today's youth have what it takes to change the world, but can only succeed if they encounter people along their path who are capable of channelling their ambitions and making the most out of their skills and contribution. The managers I have had throughout my professional career were not extraordinary when compared to today's standard, but they enabled me just enough to significantly influence my path. Of course, growing up, I was not focused on changing the world. Gen Z are! Imagine how much you can accomplish if you truly invest yourself in mentoring and guiding them!

If nothing else, I hope to leave you with this: **the world needs you to drive positive change**. And the way you interact with those around you makes all the difference in the world.

"We but mirror the world. All the tendencies present in the outer world are to be found in the world of our body. If we could change ourselves, the tendencies in the world would also change. As a man changes his own nature, so does the attitude of the world change towards him. This is the divine mystery supreme. A wonderful thing it is and the source of our happiness. We need not wait to see what others do."

— Mahatma Ghandi

EVERY
GENERATION WANTS

To feel valued

To be recognized and appreciated

To have supportive managers

To have inspiring leaders

To work in a friendly environment

To have the time to pursue their own interests

To spend more time with family

To be empowered

To have more flexibility in their work

To love their job

To feel secure and stable

To make an impact

Figure 54

References

3M. (n.d.). *3M'S 15% Culture.* Retrieved from https://www.3m.com. my/3M/en_MY/careers-my/culture/15-percent-culture/

A millennial who accepts constructive criticism. Now there's something I don't see often. [Digital image]. (2015). Retrieved from https://imgflip. com/i/l3wzn

Aileron. (2013). *The Facts of Family Business.* Retrieved from https:// www.forbes.com/sites/aileron/2013/07/31/the-facts-of-family-business/#5c52503d9884

Amazon. (2020). *We are all in on The Climate Pledge: net zero carbon by 2040.* Retrieved from https://blog.aboutamazon.com/sustainability/ we-are-all-in-on-the-climate-pledge-net-zero-carbon-by-2040

Araya, D. (2020). *The Revolution After The Crisis.* Retrieved from https:// www.forbes.com/sites/danielaraya/2020/03/31/the-revolution-after-the-crisis/#58e3b81c101e

Bakker and Oerlemans. (2011). *A Two-dimensional View of Work-related SWB.* Retrieved from https://www.researchgate.net/figure/A-two-dimensional-view-of-work-related-SWB-adapted-from-Russell-1980_ fig2_265760317

Bosch. (n.d.). *Driving Innovation.* Retrieved from https://www.bosch.com. sg/news-and-stories/driving-innovation-in-the-workplace/

Broslawsky, N. (2019). *The Right Manager.* Retrieved from https://www. nathanbroslawsky.com/blog/the-right-manager

Cain, A. (2018). *The progression of office culture from the 50s to today.* Retrieved from https://www.businessinsider.com.au/office-culture-then-and-now-2018-5

Carlson, B. (2020). *5 companies now make up 18% of the S&P 500. Is that a recipe for a crash?.* Retrieved from https://fortune.com/2020/02/11/s-and-p-500-stocks-microsoft-apple-amazon-google-facebook/

Cisco. (2020). *Cisco Innovation Challenge 2020.* Retrieved from https://cisco.innovationchallenge.com/cisco-global-problem-solver-challenge-2020

DDI World. (2018). *Global Leadership Forecast 2018.* Retrieved from https://www.ddiworld.com/research/global-leadership-forecast-2018

DoSomething Strategic. (2018). *Gen Z Puts Brands on Notice: They're Expecting More from CEOs, Companies, and Capitalism.* Retrieved from https://www.prnewswire.com/news-releases/gen-z-puts-brands-on-notice-theyre-expecting-more-from-ceos-companies-and-capitalism-300648699.html

Dyson Institute. (n.d.). *An Exceptional Degree.* Retrieved from https://www.dysoninstitute.com/the-degree/

Economic Policy Institute. (2019). *The Productivity-Pay Gap.* Retrieved from https://www.epi.org/productivity-pay-gap/

Fiedler, F.E. and Garcia, J.E. (1987). *New approaches to leadership: Cognitive resources and organizational performance.* NY: Wiley.

Fisher, A. (2019). *Yes, You Can Find a Good Job Without a College Degree.* Retrieved from https://fortune.com/2019/08/14/find-a-good-job-without-a-college-degree/

Focardi, R. (2017). *What Workers Want.* Retrieved from https://www.hrotoday.com/news/talent-acquisition/what-workers-want/

Focardi, R. (2018). *The increasing importance of "Life Careerism" in Asia.* Retrieved from https://www.linkedin.com/pulse/increasing-importance-life-careerism-asia-rachele-focardi/

Focardi, R. (2018). *The race for the next generation of talent: Gen Z in Indonesia most likely to join the workforce instead of pursuing a formal University degree*. Retrieved from https://www.linkedin.com/pulse/generation-z-indonesia-most-likely-select-alternate-path-focardi/

Focardi, R. (2019). *How Parenting Styles Affect Workplace Leadership (and Harmony)*. Retrieved from https://www.linkedin.com/pulse/how-parenting-styles-affect-workplace-leadership-harmony-focardi/

Francis, T. and Hoefel, F. (2001). *'True Gen': Generation Z and its implications for companies*. Retrieved from https://www.mckinsey.com/industries/consumer-packaged-goods/our-insights/true-gen-generation-z-and-its-implications-for-companies

Gilbert, B. (2020). *Microsoft to reportedly allow its 150,000 employees to work from home permanently, the latest tech giant to do so*. Retrieved from https://www.msn.com/en-us/money/other/microsoft-will-reportedly-allow-employees-to-work-from-home-permanently-the-latest-tech-giant-to-do-so/ar-BB19RwyW?ocid=anaheim-ntp-feeds

Glynn, N. (2012). *Ownership and management transition in a family business*. Retrieved from https://www2.deloitte.com/content/dam/Deloitte/ie/Documents/Tax/2012_succession%20planning_management_deloitte_ireland.pdf

Haden, J. (2019). *Here's How Google Knows in Less Than 5 Minutes if Someone Is a Great Leader*. Retrieved from https://www.inc.com/jeff-haden/heres-how-google-knows-in-less-than-5-minutes-if-someone-is-a-great-leader.html

Howe, N. (n.d.) *Meet Mr. and Mrs. Gen X: A New Parent Generation*. Retrieved from https://www.aasa.org/SchoolAdministratorArticle.aspx?id=11122

Howe, N. and Strauss, W. (2007), *The Next 20 Years: How Customer and Workforce Attitudes Will Evolve*. Retrieved from https://hbr.org/2007/07/the-next-20-years-how-customer-and-workforce-attitudes-will-evolve

Kairos Society. (n.d.). *A Global Community of Young Entrepreneurs.* Retrieved from https://www.kairossociety.nl

L'Oreal. (2019). *L'Oreal Brandstorm 2019.* Retrieved from https://www.loreal.com/en/news/human-relations/loreal-brandstorm-2019/

Langan-Riekhof, M., Avanni, A.B. and Janetti, A. (2017). *Sometimes the world needs a crisis: Turning challenges into opportunities.* Retrieved from https://www.brookings.edu/research/sometimes-the-world-needs-a-crisis-turning-challenges-into-opportunities/

Lev, B. (2005). *Intangibles: Management, Measurement, and Reporting.* Washington, D.C.: Brookings Institute Press.

Lorenz, T. (2019). *'OK Boomer' Marks the End of Friendly Generational Relations.* Retrieved from https://www.nytimes.com/2019/10/29/style/ok-boomer.html

Musk, E. [elomusk]. (2020, February 3). A PhD is definitely not required. All that matters is a deep understanding of AI & ability to implement NNs in a way that is actually useful (latter point is what's truly hard). Don't care if you even graduated high school [Tweet]. Retrieved from https://twitter.com/elonmusk/status/1224089444963311616?lang=en

O'Rourke, P.J. (n.d.). *How the Boomers Saved Everything.* Retrieved from https://www.aarp.org/politics-society/history/info-11-2013/wealthy-educated-spoiled-baby-boomers.html

Oh, you're a Baby Boomer? Please tell me more about how terrible my generation is. [Digital image]. (n.d.) Retrieved from http://www.quickmeme.com/meme/36835c

One Yong World (n.d.) *The Global Forum for Young Leaders.* Retrieved from www.oneyoungworld.com

OK Boomer. (2019). *In Dictionary.com.* Retrieved from https://www.dictionary.com/e/slang/ok-boomer/

Patagonia. (n.d.). *We're Part of a Movement for Change.* Retrieved from https://www.patagonia.com/activism/

Procter & Gamble. (2021). *P&G CEO Challenge*. Retrieved from https://www.pg-ceochallenge.com

PwC. (2018). *22nd Annual Global CEO Survey*. Retrieved from https://www.pwc.com/gx/en/ceo-survey/2019/report/pwc-22nd-annual-global-ceo-survey.pdf

PwC. (2019) *23rd Annual Global CEO Survey*. Retrieved from https://www.pwc.com/gx/en/ceo-agenda/ceosurvey/2020.html

Raises the next generation by spoiling them. Says generation is entitled. [Digital image]. (n.d.). Retrieved from http://www.quickmeme.com/meme/3t6rfn

Rising. (2015). *Millennials at a Glance, 2015*. Retrieved from https://www.risingms.com/wp-content/uploads/2015/12/NWC-2015-Session-Millennial-Stats.pdf

Satariano, A. (2020). *How My Boss Monitors Me While I Work From Home*. Retrieved from https://www.nytimes.com/2020/05/06/technology/employee-monitoring-work-from-home-virus.html?smtyp=cur&smid=fb-nytimes&fbclid=IwAR25Of7rxaZqeNomYIfkxdYCqKbeeGbPMUIE5h9JhPqMDrV6OE_THs7A1xg

Says nothing in life is free. Wants to pay you in experience. [Digital image]. (n.d.) Retrieved from http://www.quickmeme.com/meme/3pbwc6

Shore, N. (2012). *Turning On The "No-Collar" Workforce*. Retrieved from https://www.mediapost.com/publications/article/170109/turning-on-the-no-collar-workforce.html#ixzz1qrN7aESX

Siemens. (2020). *Siemens to establish mobile working as core component of the "new normal"*. Retrieved from https://press.siemens.com/global/en/pressrelease/siemens-establish-mobile-working-core-component-new-normal

Stein, J. (2013). *Millennials: The Me Me Me Generation*. Retrieved from https://time.com/247/millennials-the-me-me-me-generation/

Tang, S.K. (2019). *Singapore rolls out national strategy on artificial intelligence for 'impactful' social, economic benefits.* Retrieved from https://www.channelnewsasia.com/news/singapore/singapore-national-strategy-ai-economic-benefits-heng-swee-keat-12089082

Tappero, J. (n.d.). *How are Baby Boomers Affecting the Workplace.* Retrieved from https://www.westsoundworkforce.com/how-are-baby-boomers-affecting-the-workplace/

Thiefels, J. (2019). *5 Benefits of Having a Multigenerational Family Business.* Retrieve from https://www.forbes.com/sites/nextavenue/2019/01/08/5-benefits-of-having-a-multigenerational-family-business/#1a0395355247

Tolbize, A. (2008). *Generational Differences in the Workplace, University of Minnesota.* Retrieved from https://rtc.umn.edu/docs/2_18_Gen_diff_workplace.pdf

Unilever. (2020). *Unilever sets out new actions to fight climate change, and protect and regenerate nature, to preserve resources for future generations.* Retrieved from https://www.unilever.com/news/press-releases/2020/unilever-sets-out-new-actions-to-fight-climate-change-and-protect-and-regenerate-nature-to-preserve-resources-for-future-generations.html

Universum. (2006-2008). *Universum Talent Survey.* Retrieved from www.universumglobal.com

Universum. (2015). *Gen Z – The Next Generation of Talent.* Retrieved from www.universumglobal.com

Universum. (2018). *2020 Outlook – The Future of Employer Branding.* Retrieved from www.universumglobal.com

Universum. (n.d.). *Career Profiles, Universum's Talent Survey.* Retrieved from www.universumglobal.com and https://careertest.universumglobal.com/

Walker, K. [Kent_Walker]. (2020, July 13). In our own hiring, we will now treat these new career certificates as the equivalent of a four-year degree for related roles [Tweet]. Retrieved from https://twitter.com/Kent_Walker/status/1282677443652976642?s=20

World Economic Forum. (2018) *The Future of Jobs Report 2018.* Retrieved from http://www3.weforum.org/docs/WEF_Future_of_Jobs_2018.pdf

World Economic Forum. (2020). *Jobs of Tomorrow Mapping Opportunity in the New Economy.* Retrieved from http://www3.weforum.org/docs/WEF_Jobs_of_Tomorrow_2020.pdf

XYZ@Work. (2020). *Multigenerational Workforce Study.* Retrieved from https://www.xyzatwork.com/publications

Yaia. (n.d.). *Generation X Definition.* Retrieved from http://generationx.yaia.com/definition.html

Index